CW01305113

# 31019 – A FRANK ACCOUNT

# 31019 – A FRANK ACCOUNT

Frank Cheney

Book Guild Publishing
Sussex, England

First published in Great Britain in 2006 by
The Book Guild Ltd,
25 High Street,
Lewes, East Sussex
BN7 2LU

Copyright © Frank Cheney 2006

The right of Frank Cheney to be identified as the author of this work has been asserted by him in accordance with the Copyright, Designs and Patents Act 1988.

All rights reserved. No part of this publication may be reproduced, transmitted, or stored in a retrieval system, in any form or by any means, without permission in writing from the publisher, nor be otherwise circulated in any form of binding or cover other than that in which it is published and without a similar condition being imposed on the subsequent purchaser.

Typesetting in Times by
IML Typographers, Birkenhead, Merseyside

Printed in Great Britain by
CPI Bath

A catalogue record for this book is available from
The British Library.

ISBN 1 85776 978 3

# Contents

| | | |
|---|---|---|
| | Foreword | vii |
| 1 | Prelude to War | 1 |
| 2 | And So to France | 7 |
| 3 | Dunkirk | 11 |
| 4 | Lille | 17 |
| 5 | Enghien, Belgium | 29 |
| 6 | Obermassfeld, Germany | 33 |
| 7 | Stalag IXc, Bad Sulza | 37 |
| 8 | Rouen | 41 |
| 9 | Stalag VIIIb, Lamsdorf, Upper Silesia | 45 |
| 10 | Return Ticket | 69 |
| 11 | *SS Drottningholm* | 75 |
| 12 | Home Station | 81 |
| | Postscript | 87 |

## *Foreword*

Many stories have been written of daring escapes from prisoner-of-war camps by able-bodied persons; but this is the story of one of those wounded who had no chance of escape, but had simply to survive – and did so with determination and a sense of humour.

This true account is dedicated to the Bits and Pieces.

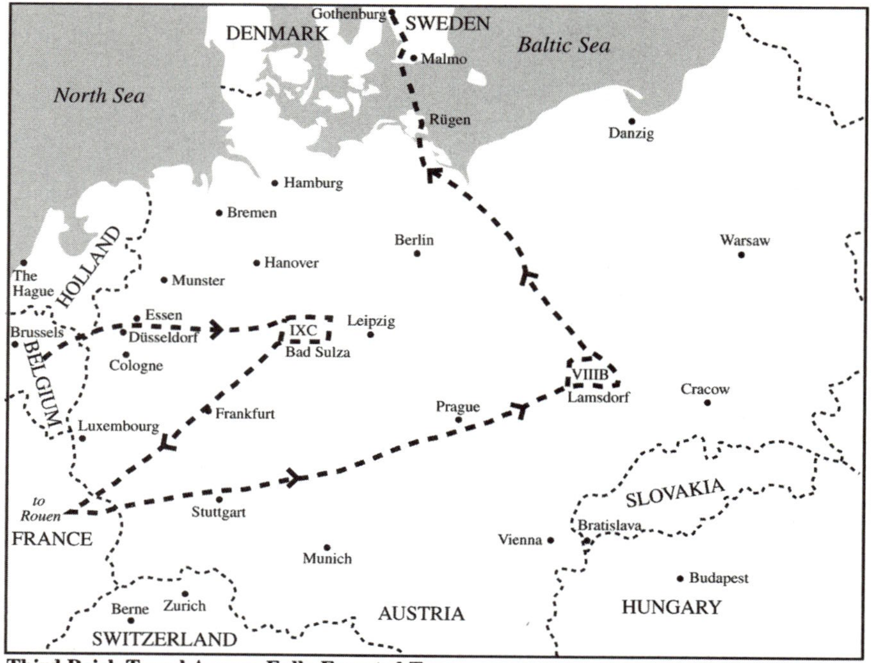

**Third Reich Travel Agency Fully Escorted Tour**
**Lille - Bad Sulza (IXC) - Rouen - Lamsdorf (VIIIB) - Sassnitz, Isle of Rügen**

# 1

## *Prelude to War*

Like a spreadeagled letter Y, the railway line and sidings dwarfed the small, very irregularly shaped field. It was just possible for a medium-sized football pitch to be marked out in the area, but it was now summer, the summer of 1939, the last week of June.

The grass in the field was shoulder high, except for the bare patches which represented the goal area of the football pitch. In the field were three youths dressed in athletic track suits and carrying spiked running shoes. Two carried sickles: their ages 19 and 20 years.

After some discussion, illustrated by arm waving, two began to cut the grass, so that there appeared a shorn path, two feet or so wide, from one straight edge of the pitch round a large semicircular curve which joined the other side of the football pitch. While the two wielded sickles and cut their track, the third peeled off his track suit and began jogging around the newly formed path. The evening training session had begun.

In spite of a lack of facilities they were very serious about their athletics, and had achieved moderate success at various sports meetings around the Home Counties. Prizewinners in those amateur days were rewarded in kind, not cash, so they would come away with something like a clock, a hall clothes-brush set or a barometer to show for their efforts.

One of them held the Bucks junior championship for the mile, and they also had some success as members of the relay team. The track was not ideal for running, being very uneven and on an incline, with the lower end very boggy. The boys, however, were not worried, and in between laps and time trials discussed the forthcoming events and the possibility of selection for the Olympics, which were due for Tokyo in the summer of 1940 – a long time away for the unsuspecting lads galloping around.

War rumblings were already being heard and two of the three were to register for conscription the next week, with a promised six months in a branch of the Armed Forces. This was not viewed with any seriousness, being looked upon as a building-up session and extended training for the precious running.

Towards the end of August 1939 the Territorial Army was called up, and one of the three was transported to Newbury racecourse for duty. Something had gone wrong – it was not at all as envisaged some months earlier!

On Sunday 3rd September 1939 war was declared. The thought was 'How long is this war going to last?'

On lst January 1940 the second lad made his way from Bletchley station to High Wycombe – via Aylesbury – to the recruiting centre. Once there, and after a medical examination, he made a voluntary attestation for the Royal Engineers.

Some months later the last of the three lads joined the Royal Air Force.


It was a bitterly cold day, 1st January, when the second lad made his way to High Wycombe. On arrival at his destination he asked the way to the recruiting centre, and as he walked through the streets the first flurries of snow began to fall. Reaching the old church hall, which had been requisitioned for military use, he pushed the door open to be met by a blast of hot air fighting to leave its confined premises. The door closed behind him and he entered a hall reeking of tobacco smoke. At one side a round Cannon stove bubbled with joy at being stoked to capacity, and was nearly at bursting point. Close by were a table and a chair, and further along in a neat row, more chairs.

The recruiting sergeant was filling his pipe, and at the same time warming the seat of his trousers.

'Yes?' he enquired between puffs, pressing down the tobacco in the bowl of the pipe and applying a match to it.

'I've come to join the Royal Engineers.'

'Sit over there.'

The train from the London terminus was crowded, punctuated here and there by a few people in uniform. In my compartment were two sergeant majors who were talking together, and by their conversation I gathered that they were bound for the same place as me – Clacton-on-Sea. I also discovered that the object was to form the recruits (all tradesmen) into companies, and as soon as possible to embark for France. This came as a great shock to me – I had never been further than Southend!

As we alighted from the train on to Clacton station, I continued chatting to the chap who had been sitting beside me. Like me, he wore glasses, and we along with hundreds of others made our way to the ticket barrier. We were greeted by a bitterly cold east wind which picked up each piece of debris and whisked it round in vicious spirals.

'All recruits for the Royal Engineers fall in over there on the right,' boomed the sergeant standing a few yards from the gate. The second cold blast in a few moments!

The column duly formed, we set off down the road. From the poster with the smiling suntanned girl in a swimsuit blazed *Welcome to Clacton!* Eventually the column of assorted personalities shuffled through the gates of Butlins Holiday Camp and on to a dusty quadrangle surrounded by barbed wire and gated, to be addressed by an officer. We would be allocated to the chalets and after we had made ourselves 'at home' we were to report to the mess room (the camp dining hall) when we would be given a meal.

My newly found friend, whose name I discovered to be Smith, and I, managed to get ourselves fitted into the same lodgings, where we proceeded to investigate the delights of a holiday camp chalet. This consisted of a room approximately ten feet by eight feet, with two single unmade beds, a wardrobe and a wash basin complete with two taps – hot and cold water. However, when I turned on the taps no water was forthcoming – it was frozen!

The cold weather intensified and with only civilian clothing one felt very cold, especially as there was no heating in the chalet. Those who could afford the ticket price for the local cinema went there to get some warmth, but privates were paid two shillings a day and there was a deduction of seven shillings a week if they were married. If you were able to go to the 'flicks' the dialogue was obliterated by the constant coughing of the soldiers, though I understand the cinema was usually very full. The bedclothes – blankets – were hardly sufficient to keep out the cold, and in the mornings those near the head bore a hoar frost where one's breath had frozen ... Eventually uniforms arrived and I had a new suit – a khaki suit!

Towards the end of January I was allowed a weekend pass to go home, and during that weekend we had a two-foot covering of snow.

Equipment was still arriving, also rifles and ammunition. The rifles were from the 1914–18 war, Lee Enfields, full of grease. We had no rifle drill or pack drill. The weather was still bitter and snow was still lying around. I think it was about the 20th February that I picked up a cold. This developed into what was probably bronchitis, so much so that my colleague reported me sick to the sergeant major. He in turn found a stretcher from somewhere and I was carted off to the medical room, and placed on the floor while the medics examined me. The verdict – 'Very bad cold, fit for duty!' I got off the stretcher, put some clothes on and walked off – coughing.

A couple of days later we were ordered to be on parade at a specific time with full dress and equipment. For daytime departures a band was on parade to play the company out. We left during the night – no band, just plenty of snow. After some considerable time, cold and with cut shoulders where the straps of the back pack had cut into the flesh, we entrained.

The compartment was lovely and warm. Soon I was dozing but coughing so much that one of my fellow-travellers said to those awake that I should have reported sick. My friend told him of the visit to the medical room and the result. There were a few unprintable words said about that!

When I awoke, the train was chugging along. The conversation had increased as a number of the other passengers had also woken. They were talking about the stop the train had made during the night, and I was asked, 'You live in Bletchley, don't you?'

'Yes,' I said.

'Oh, pity you were asleep, we stopped for about ten minutes in the station.'

Eventually we reached Southampton and embarked on one of the ferries.

# 2

## And So to France

The hold where we were was exceedingly hot. I was still unfit and I just found a spot and was 'away' again, insensible. We seemed to be stationary for a considerable time, when finally the engines started and continued running for some hours. We had no idea what was happening or where we were. Then the engines stopped: all was still. Then chains rumbling through the capstan could be heard. 'We are tying up,' someone said, and it proved to be correct. We were now in French waters and in harbour.

The train arrived at Lille La Madalaine station, where we, with our equipment, were unloaded, and we proceeded to our HQ at a small place where the Lille–Roubaix tram stopped – Plage Epinois.

We had left our lorry/truck and we, that is HQ Section, were in complete darkness in the middle of what appeared to be a road. We had stopped while some people were sent into their billet. Just after we had turned a sharp corner, a vehicle came whistling round this corner, scattering the troops. I saw from the dimmed car lights what I thought to be a path in front of the house, so I made quickly towards it, only to fall into a very large deep ditch. Somewhat shaken (but not stirred!) it took me some moments to realise what had happened. Fortunately some of the lads had caught a glimpse of me disappearing into the ditch and they hauled me out, together with my rifle. I was somewhat cold – the ditch was half full of wet snow. Oh to be in England now that April's there! But we were not: we were in France.

Next stop our billet, a small house with a bedroom larger than the rest of the rooms. It was decided that by using the bedstead and the two spring mattresses that it had (the mattresses were of small mesh wire joined at the head of the bedstead and likewise at the foot, with a gap of some nine inches separating the two) we could cope. This meant two on the floor on one side of the bed, two on the bed, and two on the floor on the other side. Each night was spent at a different site, moving clockwise around the room – just like the Mad Hatter's tea party.

The Company Office was in a very nice house on the main Lille–Roubaix boulevard opposite the tram stop. An estaminet was practically next door. Madame served excellent egg and chips, which we sampled often.

The daily routine proceeded quietly and there was a rumour that leave could start soon. My companions discovered that my birthday was in April, which caused a lot of leg-pulling. The rumours were correct and leave was arranged. They must have decided to ask the sergeant if I could go home first as this birthday was my 21st. Having got my bits and pieces together, I was ready for the transport, but before I left the rest of the office personnel, namely the two draughtsmen Creber and Price, Hale, Underdown, Merrill, and Bottomley from Dewsbury, presented me with a silver cigarette case with their good wishes. Their names were inscribed under the heading *From the Boys in the B.E.F. to Frank on his 21st birthday.*

I now had a much valued cigarette case.

About halfway through my leave the Germans entered Belgium. My leave finished, I returned to my unit in France.

The company was 'standing to'.

The people of Belgium were leaving their homes with what possessions they could carry, using any transport they could find – cart, handcarts, prams, bicycles. It was terrible to see them going with their few belongings, just anywhere to get away.

# 3

## *Dunkirk*

The company was divided in two; I was in the first half and we set off on foot towards Dunkirk, several stops being made for rest periods. The nearer we got to Dunkirk the larger the plumes of smoke rising from the burning oil dumps, huge columns of dense smoke. And the nearer we got the more shelling we got. We were also digging slit trenches, though we would not have lasted long with one clip of ammunition per man.

On reaching the outskirts of the town, the officer decided we should take shelter in the cellars of several houses, and gave the order to remain there until otherwise instructed. The next morning we were awaiting instructions but none were forthcoming. We had a full corporal in our midst, so he was asked for instructions as to what to do. 'Well, Corp? You're in charge!'

Eventually we moved off and found ourselves on the beach. It was a lovely sunny day, 26th May 1940. On the beach were several ack-ack guns – spiked – their gun barrels pointing to the sky, resembling the empty skins of giant bananas.

It was decided to move away from the beach towards the docks in the hope of finding some transport. In so doing we, a dozen or so men, found ourselves in a wooded copse at the top of one of the roads leading to the docks. It was difficult to know exactly where we were, we had no maps whatsoever.

The sound of approaching aircraft stopped the discussions and we quickly adopted the prone position. A young chap from the cookhouse and I had been talking up to that point. We were close to a very large tree. He went down next to one side of the tree and I the other.

The planes were now quite close. I had raised my head and suddenly down in all the waste material I spotted a pin. Yes, the sort used in needlework. I picked it up and said, 'Lucky pin, lucky – you know the old saying: "See a pin and pick it up, all that day you'll have good luck."'

By this time the planes had loosed their bombs and one was rapidly coming straight for me. I said to the pin, 'pins are never lucky for me!' and flicked it away. At that point the bomb veered off course as if deflected.

All the bombs landed in our vicinity. The first hit I had was shrapnel striking the underside of the left flange of my tin hat and giving me a very sharp knock on the side of the head. Almost immediately another piece hit my left foot and another hit me in the buttocks. The planes passed over. I for some reason turned over on to my back. The blood was flowing down my face. Suddenly from somewhere a 'squaddy' was bending over me and talking.

'Where's your field dressing?'

'In the pocket of the trousers, right-hand side,' I replied.

'No, it's not there, I'll use mine.'

He was using his, which is NOT recommended. Now, if he was hurt he had no field dressing.

I had just turned over when more Stukas were diving on us. My right side collected hits in the right groin and a large piece in the right thigh. During the attack my unknown friend had lifted my head and shoulders and covered me with his own body. A very brave man. I don't think he was hurt then.

After the planes had left he surveyed the damage and said, 'I'll go and find an ambulance.' When he came back and said, 'I've found a bloody ambulance,' I thought he was swearing.

He knelt down again and I asked him if my cookhouse friend, George, was all right behind the tree.

'I'll go and see.'

He came back and said, 'He's dead.'

He was away again for a few minutes, then reappeared with someone else and a stretcher. They loaded up the ambulance with other casualties and proceeded to find the hospital.

'Which way to the hospital, mate?' I heard him shout to someone.

We – the ambulance – reached a building which I presumed was a hospital and were offloaded by someone. Whether it was my very gallant gentleman I don't know. He appeared silently and vanished in the same way. I have always hoped that he got back home safely.

I was placed in a line of occupied stretchers in what I thought was a corridor. I was thirsty, as were some others in the line, some British, some French, but alas nothing was forthcoming. Then I presume that I fell asleep. I came to the next day to the sound of movement of stretchers. Soon it was my turn. Off we went, two strong men and me, the layabout! We turned into a large hall full of people, mostly stretcher-borne, and I was placed in a vacant space on the floor. I was trying to take in my surroundings when a young lady came and knelt down at the foot of the stretcher. I thought she was about my age. When she saw the state of me her expression changed to one of horror. I was stuck to the canvas by the blood from the wounds. She held a pair of scissors: her look and actions implied 'Where do I start?' I signed to her, using my fingers in a scissor movement to cut up the leg of my blood-stained trousers. The next move was to the operating theatre for a 'clean-up'.

I woke up in the hospital ward. In the bed next to the wall was a Frenchman. He must have asked the orderly what nationality I was because he called out to me.

'Are you Tommy Atkins from England?'

'Yes,' I answered.

Over the next few days he spoke to me in the English he had learnt by listening to the British radio broadcasting dance band music by Henry Hall, Joe Loss and others. The poor chap was badly wounded. He was unable to lie on his back because he had what appeared to me, when I saw the orderly attending to him, a burn from his right shoulder across his back to the left arm, touching the waist. His English was the only English I heard for some time, and as I did not speak French communication was difficult. I was again placed on a stretcher and taken to the operating theatre for another clean-up, mainly to my left foot. The initial dressing was around the ankle and instep to the toes. This time the cleaning strips had gone around the shin and part of the calf muscle. When I came to again I had been moved to another ward.

On awakening I found myself in a different atmosphere, with two British neighbours, one Welsh and one Irish Guards sergeant. I was in the middle. The RC padre visited the three of us to enquire about our general state and whether there was any way in which he could help. I said that my paybook was in the pocket of my tunic and could he possibly find it. He took down the details and said he would do his best. I was rather keen to get it back as there was a ten-shilling note tucked inside, but I had little hope of it being found among the mountains of blood-stained uniforms. However, a couple of weeks later he came to visit and said to me, 'Good news! I have your paybook.'

We were surprised one day to see three German front line troops appear and approach us. 'English?' they asked, then in German came the now familiar words, 'For you the war is over!' They handed round cigarettes and lit them. 'We have been looking for English,' one said as they left.

The hospital, we learned, was in Zuydcote, and was a

French naval sanatorium. All the nurses in this part were French and of some religious order, with black flowing gowns and shoulder capes. On their heads were huge white starched caps, shaped like a manta ray without the tail.

The time was probably around the middle of June, 11th–14th. The nun with the large hat would come and carry out the inspection and dressing of my wounds. The usual treatment of my left foot was soaking of surgical spirit, or if none was available, methylated spirit. There seemed to be a large amount of pus forming around the dressing.

Towards the end of June it was hinted that we were going to move again – destination unknown.

# 4

## *Lille*

On 1st July we were gathered together ready for ambulances. My left leg was oozing particularly white oily-type pus, when my lady with the large white headgear came round. The bandage was soaked, so she applied another on top. I was eventually put into an ambulance and from the stretcher I saw that the vehicle had solid tyres. My thoughts turned to bumpy roads and as I was slid into my vintage transport I gave myself a little talking to – 'Now remember that you are English and you are to be good!'

We duly left Zuydcote hospital and set off to who knew where. We were going along quite nicely, getting a few bumps now and then, but as time wore on into the journey so the bumps increased. Gradually the groans from the injured drowned the road noises: the further we went the louder the sounds. My left leg was now really causing me agony, and I was having great difficulty in keeping the pledge I had made before the journey started. In the end I capitulated and screamed. The scream let out the pent-up tension, until the next time. The journey seemed endless and it seemed we had been travelling for days. Suddenly the noise, the bumps and the screams stopped. *What now? Where are we?*

The door of the ambulance opened and I felt a movement as the stretchers were pulled out. Another person came to the side and assisted until the handles of the stretchers appeared.

During this operation there was considerable chatter in what sounded like French, between the men.

Now clear of the vehicle, we entered into what seemed to be a hall and then, surprise surprise, began to mount the stairs. After two or three steps I realised that we were climbing a spiral staircase. My head was behind the leading carrier as we went round. The stairs seemed quite steep, about 40–45 degrees. The ascent was at a steady rate with the lead 'horse' going quite rapidly and the 'footman' pivoting and taking the weight. I lost count of the number of flights, but looking over the side of the stretcher I could see the drop. It was rather like a giant corkscrew but with ornate sides. My men struggled on with one or two hiccups and we all three nearly went overboard. The carriers were obviously feeling the strain, particularly 'tail-end Charlie'. Probably as well that I weighed less than 11 stone.

I don't know how long the ascent took, but it was a climb – the first time I had been mountaineering! It must have been about the sixth floor when we came to a flat area and moved off to the left through double doors. We entered a large room and immediately the men turned left, went straight for two or three strides, stopped by a bed, lowered the stretcher and placed it on the bed. The room was vast, the floor highly polished. It was full of made-up beds, all with white bedspreads, and all empty. Having deposited me, my two gallant horses left without saying a word. I heard their footsteps descending the stairs, the sound decreasing as they neared the bottom, then silence. Complete silence.

How long it stayed that way I have no idea. Then I heard footsteps at the bottom of the stairs, very distant, also voices. Gradually the sounds increased in volume and then the heads appeared over the floor – they were coming up.

Several complete bodies, all wearing white coats, they all made straight for my bed. I'm trying to think how many gathered round, possibly five, two each side and one at the foot. One began to undo the bandages on my left leg, talking all the time. The bandage had to come off, it was interwoven with the flesh. A swift tug and the dressing came off, leaving a pool of oily vari-coloured pus. That hurt! Further consultations among themselves. Nobody addressed me, only nodded. Then they departed.

Silence again. Complete eerie silence. Just think, if instead of throwing that pin away that I found in the copse, I had obeyed the old rhyme and picked it up. Now, you could have heard a pin drop.

Some time passed before I was visited again by some more white-coated men. They again began to undo the dressing on my leg. I could hear myself moaning, 'Oh not again, they just did all that!' This time there was a partial replacement of the dressing. Another silence. Again no idea of time.

Footsteps again. *How many this time?* Two French army uniforms appeared. *What are they carrying? Looks like a stretcher.* I don't know whether it was the same two who had undertaken the previous climb, but I was again loaded on to the transport. I have never decided which journey was the more perilous, the ascent or the descent. Anyway, we finally arrived at the bottom and to my surprise left the building and went out into the streets of Lille. I couldn't see any vehicular transport and my carriers didn't stop to enquire for any. As they marched through the streets, carrying me, the church bells were ringing, calling the faithful to Evensong. I think I remember going past the town hall. The clock struck six.

We passed through some gates into a building and entered a white-tiled room with a strong centre light. There were several men in white, well almost white, coats.

The stretcher was placed on the floor and people gathered round me. An examination of the left leg was made, amid conversation in French. Finally a doctor straightened up and addressed me in his best English. 'I ask you for permission to take your leg off, or you will die.'

After a very exhausting day, this was the climax. Involuntary tears welled up and I remember uttering, 'No more running!' and with that agreed with a nod of the head. A stocky, broad-shouldered orderly bent down, gently picked me up and placed me on the operating table.

I came to the next day, at least so I have always thought, and I was in a bed in the centre of the ward. I do not know if there were any other beds behind me, but an entrance door was a few yards beyond. Having recovered consciousness, for some inexplicable reason I wanted to sit up. This apparently caused the nurses great concern and they tried unsuccessfully to hold me down. They then did something which I remember very vividly – they tied me down in the bed with a sheet across my shoulders. This made me even more determined that I wanted to rise, until Bill (I think his name was King) left his bed, came over and said, 'Lie still, or you will fall and hurt yourself.'

'I only wanted to sit up,' I murmured, deflated and sleepily. I went to sleep – I wondered afterwards if I had been sedated. I do not remember if anything else took place that day.

Next morning I had some coffee and roll, was washed and tidied. All was well until mid-morning when the nurses appeared with the dressing trolley. They seemed very quiet, much quieter than at breakfast time. My turn. At this point I was propped up in bed with pillows behind me. The outer bandages were taken off, revealing my new stump. My leg had been guillotined for quickness in an emergency. It was flat at the end and over the meaty flesh was a temporary dressing of fine grease-impregnated gauze. This had to be removed after two days, so off it had to come. Up to this point I was quite happy with the proceedings, then came a swift tug at the dressing and a muffled screech from me.

Another tug and a louder cry and movement down the bed from me. I was now holding the rest of my leg up, possibly to resist any further attacks, but they continued. I couldn't stop the yells as each attack increased the pain, and with each wave of pain I got further down the bed. The attempts to remove the dressing stopped. IT WAS OFF! And me? I was down at the foot of the bed – shattered. The ladies in white eased me gently back along the bed. A fresh dressing was applied and peace regained.

Later that morning a nurse came into the ward and stopped beside my bed. She began by saying how sorry she was that she was not in the operating theatre before the operation began. She explained that she had been on duty for 36 hours non-stop and had left the theatre shortly before my arrival and fallen asleep. The operation had begun when eventually she was awakened. She spoke excellent English. As she was leaving she said she would come again the next day.

Later on, another lady came into the ward accompanied by two teenage girls. They spoke to the other British lads in the ward and finally Bill brought them to introduce them to me. The older lady he introduced as Germaine and said that all of them called her Ma. She also spoke English. Ma continued to visit regularly. About the middle of July Bill came to my bedside and told me that he and the rest of the boys were being moved to the British Medical Section, which was also in Lille. I would stay where I was for a while, and then I too would be leaving the hospital, which was called St Sauveur.

The lads left. I was now the only British person in the ward. I think Ma realised this and came in almost every day, occasionally accompanied, on a Sunday I think, by the two girls. One day she came in and set the place humming – she produced a very fine bottle of champagne (apparently to cheer the 'little boy' up). Some of the nurses were in attendance and I think one of them supervised the opening – what a ceremony! 'Here's a health unto His Majesty.

Cheers!' I don't think they knew that song. We used to sing it at school – without the champagne.

On one of Ma's visits I told her about the nurse who had visited me the day after my operation and said I had not seen her since, although she had said that she would come again. Ma then told me that she had been arrested by the Gestapo and executed, shot, for collaboration with the enemy. There was a vase of flowers in the doorway, in memoriam.

I was now getting stronger and perhaps fitter but not allowed out of bed. The wound was almost healed. Looking back over the time of the amputation up to the departure of the British lads from the hospital I must have been what the Aussies would call 'pretty crook'.

Then the day arrived when I was told in French, with the help of signs, that I was leaving the next day to go to the British. An ambulance arrived with the stretcher bearers and I was off to the University of Lille. We arrived at the gateway and were allowed in with the stretcher. The sentry on duty asked my name and checked with the details he already had. There was another British soldier who had been talking to the guard. He had a dreadful wound in the face; he had lost his left eye and his cheek bore a terrible deep scar. His left arm was in a sling.

'Hello,' he greeted me.

'Hello,' I replied.

'They told me yesterday that you were coming. You are Frank Cheney, aren't you?'

'Yes,' from me.

'I am Sergeant Tertius, Cheney. My home is in Portsmouth.'

We shook hands as best we could and were interrupted by an escort which arrived for me.

'See you tomorrow, if possible,' said the sergeant.

We met once more that I can remember.

I was taken to a small room somewhere at the rear of the

chapel, referred to as Room Six. Next day one of the medical officers came to see me and carried out an examination.

'The French carried out an emergency operation, hence the "guillotine". We'll see how you get on and if all is well we will resuture. That means we will operate to take the bone back, otherwise if it is left like that the bone will protrude beyond the skin. The skin will then be folded over in a cushion of flesh. We will see how it is in a fortnight or so.'

'Thank you, sir,' said I.

Two weeks passed and then the British stretcher bearers appeared. One said, 'Frank Cheney?' so I owned up. Off we went across the road to – guess where – the maternity hospital! Oh yes it was. It was being used as a forces hospital. As far as I know there were no ladies present. After a 'settle in' routine the MO came to check on things and said, 'We'll tidy it up tomorrow.' And off he went.

Tomorrow arrived: I was loaded up and taken to the theatre. Two officers were there, both of whom I had seen during the initiation period. One explained that due to the shortage of anaesthetics they would be using chloroform.

'Nothing to worry about,' one doctor said. The proceedings started.

I came to, back in my little bed, having experienced during the period of waking what seemed to be the splitting of the atom. Anyway, there I was tucked up in my comfortable surroundings.

After about a week my transport arrived to take me back across the road. Having loaded me up, the two bearers began to crack a few jokes about which was the correct way to go through the front door, feet or head first.

'Well, is he alive? Can't be alive, look, he hasn't moved,' and so the banter went on. One of the bearers was called Jack Victor, and we later became very good friends. On entering the chapel we were directed to the altar steps and I was placed in a vacant bed by the side of the high altar.

One morning the orderly doctor came on his rounds. (He had a particular habit of ending a sentence with 'what-what' so of course he was called Dr What-what.) He started his inspection on the altar steps on the opposite side to me, so I was 'tail-lamp Charlie'. He reached me and asked how I was.

'All right, sir.'

Then he went on to say, 'It's about time you shaved.'

There was no answer. I had nothing. I was as poor as a church mouse. That's possibly why I was at the top of the step – I had nothing. I was wearing my best birthday outfit, all nice and shiny. I had no toiletries, including no razor. But somewhere I did have a ten-shilling note.

Shortly after that it was decided to move me down to the body of the church, the nave. There were two rows of beds each side of the nave, with an empty space in the middle. I was approximately a third of the way down the row with a space of about 18 inches each side. The row behind me was cut short by protruding granite columns. There were four occupied beds in the recess: Dick Smith from Winson Green, Birmingham, Geordy Thompson and Jock Hamilton from Edinburgh, Hammy for short. Geordy was missing a leg above the knee, the other two below the knee. The fourth was Tidball from Hull, a great Yorkshireman. Next to my left was Terry, who had been in Australia growing pineapples and wanted to get back as soon as possible, another Smith, John, Sergeant Stan Burt, amputation below the knee and other foot injuries, from the Guards, Coldstreams, I think. A jolly bunch they were, particularly the four behind – like kittens, full of mischief.

Some of the citizens of Lille came into the chapel and brought items of clothing and something to eat. Tidball got friendly with a bearded gentleman who wore a black velour coat and a round trilby type hat, whom he always referred to as the Professor. As he had some French francs he got the Professor to buy some pâté for him. The order used to go in two days before delivery. Suddenly the Germans stopped the visitations, but in order to keep their contact the local citizens made up small parcels and our medical orderlies arranged 'fishing trips'. The orderlies went on the roof with string or rope, let down one end to the ground and the packages with the patients' names were hauled up. This continued until the Germans scattered the citizens from the precinct.

The evenings were long, and some of the staff and patients tried to entertain with various 'turns' to cheer us up. One favourite from an RAMC sergeant was 'Old Father Thames' sung in a rich baritone.

We were now into August and I was still confined to my bed. The friendly medical orderly who looked after our 'gang', a Cornishman named Phil Care, was somewhat concerned because I could not straighten my knee. He used to say almost daily, 'Can you straighten your leg?' Then, 'You'll have to straighten it, otherwise they won't be able to fit a new leg.'

I kept trying. Then one morning I woke and lo and behold, I could straighten the knee. Cheers! I told Phil. Together we investigated my bedding and around the knee area was wet. 'You've had an abscess,' said Phil.

One day about the end of September another of our orderlies came along with a pair of crutches. He stopped at my domain and said, 'Come along, you can get up now.'

I turned myself around with my leg over the side of the bed, and he stood in front of me, holding the crutches apart to the width of my body. His grip on each crutch tightened as he said, 'Up you get!'

I gripped the crutches, one in each hand, and he continued to grip firmly as I tried to get myself off the bed. I *could not get up*! I made several attempts but I could not rise. Involuntary tears welled up and I was in a mist, still trying.

'Have a rest,' he said.

Throughout this attempt he had been great. His face

tightened; he wanted to help me to get up but he and I knew that if he did I would never do it, and I had to do it by myself. Sitting back on the bed I was very disappointed. After a break he said, 'Have another go,' a sort of suggestion and command.

(I think my friend's name was Phil. When we spoke together before this attempt on Everest he said he would like to be an actor.)

I was still a little shaky from the previous attempt but we began again. His grip on the sticks was as firm as ever. I tried once. I tried again and then again. Was I *never* going to get up? Then suddenly something somewhere got the message – LIFT OFF. I was trying to laugh and cry at the same time, tears were running down my face, but I was UP. Phil's face remained firm as a rock as it had been throughout the proceedings. What a performance of support!

I stood up with the crutches for a while to get my balance. It seemed strange: the world took on a different meaning. We decided that I should sit down again for a short recovery period and then take a step with the crutches. This we did, he watching, correcting and coaching. After a few minutes he said, 'We will continue tomorrow.'

Having acquired an assortment of clothing and an old suede shoe, I was able soon to 'motor' under my own steam, with a big head full of confidence. Where we were situated in the nave there was a small doorway with a couple of steps down to a gritty gravel and dirt path around a grassed quadrangle. The lads used to go out into this area for some fresh air. First they had to go down the two steps. The experts put the crutches down on the path and cleared the obstacle in one swing. So what did the big-headed one do? No prizes for the answer. The novice would show them! I approached the top step, placed the crutches firmly on the path, and swung. I flew through the air in a flat swallow dive. Instinctively I folded the knee of the amputation leg and crashed down on

the path. I crawled back up the steps and was rubbing my knee when a doctor approached. It was Doctor What-what.
'Hello, what's the matter?'
'I've fallen down the steps, sir.'
'Any damage?'
'No, thank you, just a bang on my knee, sir.'
'That's all right then, what-what.' With that he left.

The reason for the fall, I discovered, was that the sticks were too short and did not go high enough to allow some gripping of the upper arms under the shoulder. Of course Phil heard about it and produced a longer pair of crutches. But I waited some time before I attempted another acrobatic swing. End of my first lesson. There would be more.

Several days later we were told that we were all moving the next day, and to be ready. The day came. I put on my best uniform, my ex-French, possibly cavalry, pantaloons, rather like plus fours for golf, and buttoned below the knee, complemented by my elegant, far from new, suede shoe. I'm not sure whether I had a sock. Thus attired, I set off for who knew where.

Lorry transport was supplied. It was some climb into the back of an army lorry, as we had to stand on the one leg that we had and somehow inch ourselves up. Usually the personnel came to the rescue of those stranded. No German assistance was offered. Probably as well!

We duly reached Lille railway station via a large square which had been cleared of traffic and people. There was a large number of German troops on duty ready for action. The citizens of Lille were behind barricades. We seemed to have a very good crowd to see us off, and there was some defiant hand waving from both sides.

All aboard, we left Lille.

# 5

## *Enghien, Belgium*

We duly arrived at a bleak-looking place with a tarmacadam square, and buildings on three sides. On the right side was a low flat building, facing was a four-storey building and on the left what appeared to be an assembly hall. We were to go inside the middle one, which was a dormitory.

Entering the building through a large doorway, one was faced with several flights of stairs. I was one of the last to reach them. Tidball, Dick Smith, Jock Hamilton and Tommo were on their way up. I got to the bottom and looked up – nothing but stairs as far as the eye could see, and I asked myself, 'How am I going to climb up there?' Calls from the mountaineers.

'Come on, Lon, it's easy!' from one voice.

'You can do it, Chain,' from another.

Then a united chorus, 'Come ON!'

By now I was standing there on my own. I looked up the long flight of stairs. I had to go – so up I went.

With one hand on the stair handrail, one crutch on the right side, hand holding the other crutch in part of the hand also holding the handle on the vertical crutch, slowly I mounted the stairs. As I went up I could hear the boys nattering away and as I finally approached the doorway I heard someone say, 'Leave that bunk for Frank.' (I was called all sorts of names).

As I came through the door someone yelled, 'Where have you been?' This was followed by shouts of laughter from the rest.

'Fishing,' I replied, 'but I couldn't get a bite.'

'There's your bunk, Lon.'

The bunks were wooden constructions resembling a squared-off letter U, and joined together to form two long rows. They were about six feet high, and had side partitions protruding four or five feet with a fixture resembling a small table. The bed was less than six feet long; somewhat cramped. Having eventually reached my new home I flopped down on the bed – hard as a board, and that's what it was.

There was a metallic noise coming from the stairway and soon there appeared two men carrying a large bin-type vessel with side handles. The contents were steaming. Tin bowls were issued. I can't remember if we had spoons, anyway, we would have found some means to consume food. Food, glorious food! Well, this wasn't anything to sing about. It seemed to be a mixture of several items: biscuits as issued to the French army, prunes, potatoes and tree leaves (that's what they were – bay leaves, I found out later. Well, my mother never used bay leaves.)

It was dark, there were no curtains or blackout at the windows and we had no light, so after a chat among the lads it was bed.

A week or so went by and I was getting used to being a mountaineer, going up and down when necessary to what had been labelled the 'parade ground'. Some of our 'news hounds' reported that their scoop was that this collection of buildings was an agricultural college and we were occupying the dormitory. The days passed into evenings and with the daylight fading very quickly we had lots of time on our hands. We had a few books in English brought with us thus far, and with the weather worsening during the day the tendency was to read while the light lasted and then gather round one or two cubicles, some people sitting on the floor or window sills. The conversation was wide ranging. Someone would make a statement or comment which would be picked up by someone else and a discussion would ensue. The favourite comments were about books and often referred to the author's description of a meal. This usually took place in a swanky hotel and consisted of a nine-course menu accompanied by fine wine. No one in the books EVER sent the fillet steak back. Rotten lot, having all that good food and us on our skimpy rations!

Probably another evening after our meagre supper, someone would remark, 'I could just do with roast beef and three veg.'

Then our friend Tidball would enter into the fray with something like, 'You have your beef and I'll have a lovely Dover sole!'

(Well, I did say he came from Hull.) And so it went on, one against the other, causing much merriment and helping the time along. Then it was off to our little shacks to dream of large steaks and Dover soles.

One day when I had made the descent to the 'parade ground', there to meet other inhabitants, the sun made a welcome appearance. While this was being enjoyed I chatted to other inmates. The question was usually, 'Where do you come from?'

When this was asked of me, I replied, 'North Buckinghamshire.'

'Whereabouts in North Bucks?'

'Fenny Stratford,' was the answer.

'Oh yes, I've been to the pictures there in the High Street. I live in Hanslope.'

He was a member of the TA and based at Wolverton. His name was Victor Payne and it was the start of a very good friendship.

Vic informed me that he was in the building on the right,

so we crossed the square and went in. It was a large place with bunks, only the base, close together with very little space between them. Vic occupied one of these. We chatted for some time, our conversation being interrupted by questions from other members of the establishment. Then it was time for me to wend my way back and 'up the wooden hill to Bedfordshire', to my tiny little bunk – it was all right on my left side – and the conversations of the gourmet diners.

We were now into December and the weather was very wintery. We then received orders to be prepared to move. The time came again to report below and be transported to the railway station. The snow began to fall as we were ushered on to the train. All aboard, and we were off, to we knew not where.

# 6

## *Obermassfeld, Germany*

The lads and I were allowed a vestibule carriage (one with table and seating for four people). We could hardly believe our luck with this unaccustomed luxury. This arrangement was different from the corridor coaches with the postern (guard) patrolling up and down. If you needed to visit the lavatory the guard had to be summoned and he would wait outside the door until you appeared again ... In the corridor coaches the sleeping arrangement would be two people on the luggage racks, one each side, two on the seats and two on the floor. Our present arrangement would have to be discussed, but there would be no difficulty. We were travelling what seemed to be short distances and then stopped, but as no looking out was allowed the reason was unknown. One evening we were 'side-lined' again and during the night heard bombing and gunfire. Good old RAF. After a very long stop, off we chugged again. We had been travelling for a while, watching the snowflakes falling silently on the surrounding countryside, then we were going through a station. Düsseldorf. (Funny, I can't remember crossing the Rhine,)

One of our chaps collected some breakfast for us, Knäckerbrot, a hard sort of biscuit, and acorn coffee. We were climbing pretty high, the engine was really puffing – probably near exhaustion! Munching the German 'hardtack' biscuit and sipping the special German coffee, it was pleasant to see the snow-covered countryside, though we were pleased not to be out in it.

After four nights on the train we were pleased to arrive at the station siding of Obermassfeld. I think it was 12th December that we reached Germany. Our new billet was a large dairy and outbuildings. One of the outbuildings had been converted into an auxilliary hospital ward, with four rows of beds and snow-white bedding. We were issued with German striped linen hospital clothes. My bed was on the right of the entrance, nearly halfway down, about 50 yards from the doorway. Our floor was reached up two short flights of steps. Reaching the top of the second flight you turned half right and entered through a double doorway set at a slight angle in the corner of the ward. Immediately on the left was a row of beds, a corridor, two rows of beds, a corridor of clear flooring, then our row of beds. The clear corridor paths led to the ablutions, the washing area. While we were wearing our hospital attire. the orderlies and officers retained their British army uniforms. At least I got rid of my theatrical outfit of bits and pieces.

Life was difficult. The cold snowy weather outside and the glaring whiteness of the wards in the building were upsetting the usual cheerful attitude of the lads and making them edgy. They were snapping and snarling at their best mates – only for seconds, but it showed. Perhaps the main cause of that attitude was that Christmas Day was fast approaching. Some of us were single, but many others had wives and children; some of the children had never seen their fathers, and the fathers had not seen those children.

So Christmas Day arrived. The whole place was very quiet; there was seldom any laughter. The food ration remained the same – awful! But around the midday meal time the British orderlies distributed a small bottle of beer together with some cigarettes to each person. It was a marvellous gesture from our officers, who had somehow managed to negotiate a deal with our jailers. Christmas time passed, but not the mood of the men.

Some of the personnel in the ward next to us used our washroom, one person in particular. According to reports he was with the Northamptonshire Regiment. On one particular day he was later than usual and the path to the ablutions was clear of people, who were all on their beds. He entered the ward through the doorway, his left arm supported by a ladder-type support about nine inches wide. It started from the waist, went straight up to the armpit, and bent under the outstretched arm and hand, the wire support covered by bandages. Over his two middle fingers was looped the string of his washing bag. He was unable to take a full stride because of an injury to his right foot, so he propelled himself forward by taking half a stride with the left and bringing the other with a dropped foot action up to the left.

He was singing to himself – 'Hearts of oak are our ships, Jolly tars are our men.'

The tune was taken up by the lads as he passed.

'We always are ready' the volume increased.

'Steady, boys, steady' – even louder.

'WE'LL FIGHT AND WE'LL CONQUER AGAIN AND AGAIN!'

And at the final crescendo the door of the washroom slammed shut and simultaneously, as if directed by the conductor's baton, the song ceased. Absolute silence!

The silence was eventually broken by an orderly entering the ward in a hurry. When he was a few yards inside he yelled, while still walking, 'Attention everybody! We have just been to the railway sidings. PARCELS HAVE ARRIVED!'

If he had anything further to say it was drowned by minutes of cheering. When it subsided he said, 'We hope to unload them as soon as possible. We don't know how many there are.'

During our stay in Obermassfeld our two doctors had started research into 'the phantom limb'. After an amputation the patients were experiencing dreams in which they still had two legs. At times during the day there was the feeling that the original leg was still there. They wrote a paper on some of their findings and it was brought back to England in 1943. It was subsequently published in a medical journal.

Having got thus far I had better say that I have omitted to tell you of a very important event. It was that of receiving my official *Kriegsgefangener* number, 31019. I was also given a piece of pliable metal substance with the number on it, to be kept about my person. I also have a new suit, a khaki suit for prisoner-of-war 31019.

# 7

## Stalag IXc, Bad Sulza

Not long after the arrival of the parcels we were moving again. This time there was no 'taxi' to the station. There were only a few of us, a dozen or so, so our taxi was our crutches. We were escorted by some of our medics, and of course the good old *Posten* (guards). Somehow we reached the 'Kriegie' camp of IXc Bad Sulza. The camp was not very big, possibly six or seven huts, wattle and daub type of construction, some 60 feet long, single floor, entrance at one end. The occupants were a mixture of nationalities, mainly French and British, with a few others. I finished up in a hut full of Frenchmen.

The wooden bunks were in stacks of three, tightly packed. The empty bunk was on top, the penthouse, with a window close by. I think some of the French had been in business and had learnt some English because they took the chance to speak to me in English whenever they could. This made things a lot easier for me, because if any orders were in French I had several interpreters.

The camp was situated on one side of a mini-mountain, on the other side was a river, and next to the river a road. On one occasion some of the RAF chaps decided to have a mock boxing tournament. The boxing ring was practically under the elevated sentry box. The contestants were doing rather well at their make-believe bout and the guard was taking a great interest in the 'tournament'.

While the boxing was in progress two of the others were slinging blankets over the top of the wire fencing. Lots of spectators were watching both the blankets and the 'boxing'. As the RAF lads began climbing, at first unnoticed into the river and wading along, some of the spectators, especially the French, in their excitement began chattering and pointing. This diverted the guard's attention from the boxing and he began bounding from one side of his platform to investigate. Suddenly a rifle shot rang out; another shout from the guard and more rifle shots. Sad to say the airmen had to surrender and put their hands up. Very quickly they were surrounded by the rest of the guards from the guardroom. Human curiosity let them down, but my word, it caused some excitement!

I was visiting one of the huts across from my quarters when I spotted a chap, a corporal, whom I thought I had seen before somewhere. I was on crutches, as was he, with a foot bandaged. Approaching him from the front I said, 'Are you in 665 Construction Company, RE?'

He nodded, and at the same time said, 'Yes.'

He was the corporal who was in charge before we were attacked by the Stukas. He said only what I have written. I would have liked to have carried on, but he moved away. We did not meet again.

There was a scoop (rumour) circulating that talks relating to repatriation of the wounded were going to take place. Some weeks previously we had welcomed several Swiss doctors and others. They had inspected the conditions of the camp; we the wounded were also examined and wounds etc. recorded into various categories. They also carried out measurements for artificial limbs. The Germans gave no help whatever on the subject of legs and arms.

It was a very nice day weather-wise, and lots of our lads were out in the open enjoying the sunshine. The main gate was being unlocked and opened and two British soldiers were pushed through, followed by armed guards. Suddenly whatever the British lads were doing stopped. All eyes were on the two newcomers. Whispering began among them and they agreed one was 'Pip' Newman, Major Philip Newman. He and his companion received a great cheer.

(Major Newman and his fellow medical officers drew lots to decide which should stay behind with the wounded after the evacuation. He drew the short straw. He had toured the French naval hospital in Zuydcote and spoken to me and my two companions, asking us about our condition. He had stood on the quay at Dunkirk as the last ship pulled away, smoking a cigarette.)

The two of them were placed in the 'cooler' for a period of solitary confinement – bread and water was the usual ration. The lads who knew the Major well through his medical services clubbed together and groceries were delivered through a small hole at the back of the clink. Happy days!

The talk now circulating in Bad Sulza was that there was to be a repatriation of prisoners-of-war, both British and German. Even the Frenchmen in my hut thought so, and said often to me that I was going home soon. Several gave me their address.

'Come and see me *après la guerre*.'

The day came with orders to pack our kit. I like that phrase; anyone would think that each of us had a Pickfords furniture van. I only had a cardboard margarine box, about 15 inches by 12.

Anyway, we were again on the move. The thought of going home was now becoming a belief. I think the German guards also believed that this escort was an easy job. They probably thought we were going home so would have no need to escape.

# 8

## *Rouen*

The train was of corridor stock. We still had *Posten* with us, but they only appeared at intervals and the nearer we approached to our destination, which we believed to be Rouen, the less we saw of them. The further we got into France the more confidence we had that we were going home, so much so that we became intoxicated by the thought.

At this time we still had odd tins of food with us. No guards were watching, so down came those windows which could be moved, and we waved to the people walking or working near the railway. Suddenly a tin was thrown out of the window and clattered along the track to be picked up by some person. It was then thought to be a great thing. Where houses were near to the tracks a barrage of tins flew through the air. The first tin struck a door, and a lady opened the door; the second likewise and the third followed. One, two, three, the tins hit the doors, the women opened the doors, looked down, saw the tins, picked them up, looked first at one, then the other, then at the sky, asking, 'Where from?' Terrific cheering came from the 'artillery' – the British were still about! Furious waving came from the French ladies. But we kept what tea we had.

The train rolled on and finally stopped at Rouen. We were transported to the cavalry barracks, and here we were housed for some time. Eventually we were informed that the 'exchange talks' had broken down.

I remember sitting on bales of straw under an open-sided storage shed, puncturing a large tin of Nestlé's condensed milk and licking it dry, along with another lad from Fenny Stratford. We had just about emptied the tin when the bugler sounded the last post. We had sat on these bales for a long time without talking very much; we could not find things to say. Slowly we made our way to the main building before the lights went out. My companion was John Plumb, who had been wounded at St Valery and lost his arm from the shoulder.

The citizens of Rouen soon found out that the British were in the barracks and tried, sometimes succeeding, to get letters and parcels to us, but the Germans cordoned the approach areas off and posted a 24-hour guard.

Not long after that about 1,200 of us were moved to the racecourse into what had been a British army camp with Nissen huts. A brick-built structure was turned into a hospital with about 12 beds and a small annexe used for minor surgery. The Nissen huts were equipped with bedboards and straw palliasses, and gradually all the bedboards were used to build fires. To replace these the 'fishermen' decided to collect all the string they could find and use it to make string hammocks.

A few days before Christmas 1941 all the people who were able to walk (this included those with arm injuries and arm amputations) were instructed to be ready to move at any time. A day or two later orders to move were given by the Germans. We had been together for some months and friends had been made. Hurried handshakes were given and 'Good luck, mates' were said.

The camp population had dwindled dramatically to

something like 250, maybe less. It was thought that the reason for the exodus was that, as we were at Rouen and in France, the distance to escape to Spain and Portugal had been greatly reduced; also that people with leg injuries and amputations would have no possibility of escaping.

I remember talking to a young Scot, a leg amputee, on one occasion. His leg had been amputated mid-thigh and he had been fitted with a French-made pylon leg. There was no joint in the wooden structure, so he walked straight-legged. During our general conversation he told me he was trying to fix a foot, or something to hold a shoe and therefore resembling a foot; and all this was to end in an escape attempt. Having had a chat we went our separate ways, but those thoughts were happy thoughts!

Christmas came and went, uncelebrated. All I remember about it was how marvellous the mistletoe looked, hanging from most of the apple trees around the racecourse. And so we entered a new year, 1942. It arrived very silently and unannounced.

Life in the camp drifted on, and then about 26th January, things happened. We had among our attendant medical orderlies a number of Australians and New Zealanders. They obviously decided that their services could be better used elsewhere, also that their location was a good place from which to go 'walkabout', being halfway to the coast. On the night they decided to make this attempt, all was going well until the air raid siren sounded. It was understood that about 30 people had escaped, including Hamish Gunn, the Scots lad I had been talking to. The tail-enders had a difficult job to hide but most of the 30 were out.

Now there was hell on: a bloody air raid and escapers all at once! No further comment.

Next morning roll-call started at 7 a.m. and went on for hours, check-count after check, then the missing number was agreed.

Several days later we left Rouen and its sunshine to travel to who knew where.

# 9

## *Stalag VIIIb, Lamsdorf, Upper Silesia*

Transport to the railway station was by army vehicle. We were then ushered into the carriages through a corridor of armed guards spaced about ten feet apart. The carriage stock was similar to the train that brought us to Rouen, with corridors, so we sorted ourselves out, under supervision of course. There was *not* going to be another attempt to escape. I suppose it would have been about 11 o'clock when we actually began our journey. The 'scoop' was that Stalag VIIIb was the probable destination, also that it was in punishment for the breakout. Some of our lads had been in Lamsdorf before coming on the 'repatriation special' and were not looking forward to going back there – a minor fortress.

If I remember correctly, we were seven nights on the train before we eventually stopped at wherever our destination was. We guessed it was our destination because of the rushing around by the Germans.

'It's Lamsdorf VIIIb,' said one of the former occupants.

Alighting from the train, we found a sullen sky, a rough wind, flakes of snow and freezing cold. Welcome to Lamsdorf, the supreme holiday camp of *Deutschland*! The gateway into the camp had snow, and where vehicles had passed, the snow had been compounded and then frozen. In this icy light, together with the light from what could have been the guardroom, the very wheel marks glistened. With great caution, me with my margarine box on my back, we made our way along this cart track road to our compound, Block 4. Block 4 was surrounded by high barbed wire after that 'banjo' wire and after that another high wire, about seven feet by seven feet in all. Inside the compound were four barrack huts, about a hundred yards long, possibly longer, with an entrance door on the side which had the appearance of an afterthought. In two or three strides you were inside the foyer. On your left was the door to the living and sleeping quarters; opposite was the night latrine. As you entered the living area, on the left were several rows of wooden bunks; in the middle, and spaced several yards apart, were stout wooden columns about a foot square. Proceeding across the width of the hut you came to a continuous row of coat hanger pegs, and finally some 20 feet from the coat hangers to the outer wall was what might be called 'open planning': tables spaced the length of this section together with wooden forms. The two sections of the hut, each a mirror image of the other, were divided by the ablutions washhouse. The day latrine was a large purpose-built structure to serve all the four huts. Our hut was 11B, the other end 11A.

Before arriving at Hut 11B we had a long way to go along the carriageway. The high wind was picking up the debris and twisting it round in spirals, rather like the windy scenes in some desolate cowboy town. A gust of wind, and the spirals would take off. This made the use of crutches somewhat difficult. The depth of snow was variable. Having extracted the crutches, sometimes one at a time, from the snow, I swung them forward and put them down over the next patch of ground, but sometimes a single crutch would find a soft patch of snow and down it would go. Never say die ... Keep going ... I duly reached my new residence, found an unoccupied bunk, subsided on it, pushed my margarine box under the bed and pondered – what now?

I have often wondered what did take place after the period of relaxation. Did we have any bedding? Were there any lights on? Was there any heating or any food available? All I can remember is that in my little box I had a Red Cross blanket, given to me at some stage in our travels. Also there was no hot water – or hot water bottles.

Next day was a day for acclimatisation and bedding in, finding out where things were. We had already found one – roll-call at 7 a.m. A spot must be claimed on the table that was available and our complement was John Collins, a Scot, 'Spike' Kelly, a Scouse from Liverpool, 'Bernard' Shaw, Harry 'Smoky' Sell, Geordy, Clarence Aubert from Jersey, Willis 'Mildew' Milner and me, Frank Cheney, answering to many other titles (some unprintable). There were two table-length wooden benches. The table was approximately two feet six wide by six feet long. In the hut there was also a stove, housed in cladding of some sort, which radiated the heat from the fire, fuelled by what looked and felt like coal slack, stuck together with something similar to cement. This was moulded into small cobbles which so far seemed to burn well. We had swapped the spring weather of February in Rouen for the blizzards of Upper Silesia, not too far from Breslau.

There was another compound beyond the latrine but it appeared to be unoccupied. Beyond the barbed wire fence was yet another compound, so that made our position free from building on two sides and enclosed on the other two sides. The German guards had a small building, like a guard room, with the equivalent of our ranking sergeant. The ordinary *Posten* opened and closed the gate under orders to allow entry and exit. The gates were often locked and passage restricted.

The senior non-commissioned officer in our hut was RSM 'Bill' Cotton, a very tall man, about six foot four. I think he was from the Birmingham area. Sergeant Sadler was the compound interpreter. 'Wingy', as he was always called, spoke German fluently. His arm was amputated from the shoulder. The combined huts of 11A and 11B were thought to have housed over one hundred leg amputees.

On the second day after our arrival we received – that is, our SBO received – an invitation to both our huts to attend a band concert on the next evening in the camp theatre (a converted hut) by Stalag VIIIb Dance Band, conductor Corporal 'Jimmy' Howe. Great excitement! We braved the weather conditions and were granted permission to pass the guards, going round to the left up the cart track past the cookhouse. A little further on, we turned right and presented ourselves at the theatre. All the musicians were bandsmen, probably from military bands. They played dance music in the style of the Jack Payne orchestra, some band members doubling up and inserting comedy items to enhance the programme. After the concert we had to walk home to Block 4; alas, no buses!

The next day Lamsdorf had a different feel about it. Bandmaster James Howe had cheered us up. On his eventual return to England he remained in the army, rising to the rank of Major, Master of the Queen's Music, presenter of the music for the famous Edinburgh Tattoo. A marvellous achievement.

With the increase in daylight each day, we were able to stay outside instead of being in the hut playing cards and so on to while away the dragging time. We had no radio nor other instruments of communication, so our knowledge of what was happening in the outside world was nil. Our 'news-hounds' used to circulate rumours, but the good things promised never turned up.

A 'Kriegie' from Eastbourne who had been a headmaster in

that area had managed to persuade the camp Commandant to allow a hut, which I think was near to the theatre, to be used as a school. I believe at this time the camp had nine or ten thousand inmates. This total consisted largely of permanent residents, such as us. For instance, the four huts in our compound were occupied by over one thousand personnel who had been declared unfit for service. Lots needed medical attention but were unable to receive it. Well, we were prisoners, and the Germans had their own people to attend to. With some exceptions, like our medical officers and orderlies, all inmates had been passed by visiting Swiss medical officers.

There was another compound, referred to as the 'Working Compound'. This catered for people who were out on location such as farms, salt and coal mines. These people were returned to Lamsdorf in cases of illness or need of medical attention. We had what was referred to as the camp hospital, staffed by our British and Allied medics, very dedicated people. The working conditions for them were only about the same as 'field' conditions. The floating population of this compound was about nine hundred.

The RAF non-commissioned officers occupied a compound next to ours, their complement about the same as the Army, and there were also some Navy personnel, again about a thousand men. NCOs were, under the Geneva Convention, not allowed to work. Another compound housed the people, such as cooks, who worked in the camp itself.

We had a camp 'newspaper' giving details of forthcoming events in the theatre and the order of attendance for the various compounds, also of classes at the school. Language classes were held, Greek (classical and modern), German, French and several others. Our friend Willis Milner signed up for French and German. I undertook French. Our tutor for French was an Australian by the name of Smith who, when at home, had been a lecturer at Sydney University. There were lots of well-qualified people for lots of subjects and the college was well attended. An approach was made to Oxford University for registration as a college, and this was accepted, together with the design of a college coat of arms. This was the torch of knowledge encircled by barbed wire, below the insignia of the Red Cross and St John, with the motto *Libertas Scientiae Pacis Precursor*, and beneath the shield, *Stalag VIIIb College*. Examinations in various subjects were taken and the papers returned to England for marking.

Parading for roll-call one morning outside, we discovered that the compound next door, which had been empty, was now occupied. The new occupants were French Canadians. They had lost all their personal belongings and equipment, in many cases their clothing was in tatters Well, one could understand it – they had engaged the enemy in the raid on Dieppe. Some assistance was obviously required. We managed to collect together some toiletries, razors, blades, soap, combs – anything which would help them. These essentials were expertly despatched over the two high barbed-wire fences. I think the bowling was pretty accurate – very little fell into 'no-man's-land'.

After a week or so, when things had returned to nearly normal, the Canadians filtered into our hut. Their personal mail and parcels began to arrive. I remember two or three came into our hut carrying lids from Red Cross parcels. These were balanced very carefully, trying not to let the contents fall out. The lids contained cigarettes – 2,000 Sweet Caporal cigarettes. They began their circuit through the hut, offering the lids and contents.

'Have a cigarette,' they said, 'You helped us when we arrived without anything.'

The Germans had decided to search the parcels by tipping out the contents and opening articles. Usually several cigarettes were broken in half.

We gratefully accepted the gift, and wondered what their expression was like when the searchers saw 2,000 fags spilling into the parcel lid! Our personal cigarette parcels from Britain were usually of 200. What marvellous propaganda! The Canadians used to come round often, and when some 'soft balls' arrived, they brought the equipment with them and did their best to teach us how to play.

All was quiet for a couple of days, with no visits. They had been confined to barracks and a lot had been manacled with handcuffs and chains. This was stated to be a reprisal as some of the German troops had been found in Dieppe wearing similar handcuffs. This practice went on for some time and was eventually transferred to some of the RAF personnel. On the subject of manacles, our college had a portrait, painted by a prisoner, of a manacled Canadian. It was very well executed by the artist and I have often wondered what happened to it.

One day a set of deck quoits arrived, complete with net. After some days of practice someone suggested that we should have a competition for the champions, teams to be of two people, one with amputation above the knee and his team-mate to be a below-the-knee amputee. I can't remember how the pairing was arrived at, but my partner was 'Ginger' Powis. The court was scratched out in the dusty top-soil and by some good fortune Ginge and I reached the semi-final. Then we were in the final, set all square, going for – well, not gold. The pace was furious, the old quoit buzzing about all over the court and extraordinary feats of agility were being performed by both teams – that is, until one quoit came across the court diagonally and was about to drop in the court about five feet to my left. I lunged to the left and was in full flight with all my weight on the home-made leg when it fell to pieces.

The leg was made in the camp workshop under the direction of Sergeant Cook, always called 'Cookie'. It consisted of wood, similar to a broom handle, reaching from the knee joint to the ground, split down to about halfway and a spacer inserted and pinned to each side. It then looked like a catapult without the elastic. A leather socket was constructed, open at each end. The material was old French boot tops, cleverly stitched together. Leather loops were stitched to the socket. The wooden side supports were pushed through the leather Us and the socket nailed through the leather and into the wooden support. A canvas 'gaiter' was fixed to the top of the timber frame and this fitted around the lower thigh above the knee.

Returning to the match – I missed the quoit. Point lost, and another redskin bit the dust. An armistice was arranged while essential repairs were carried out, by finding a large stone to hammer back all the nails. It was finally agreed by the opposition that we were *very* gallant losers.

It was announced that an international football match had been planned, England versus Scotland. The football pitch was to be situated in the compound next to us. The Canadians who had occupied the premises previously had now moved on. Plans had to be made. There were no seats there. Some illustrious person wondered how we were going to get seats. Silence. Take a form from here? Well, Hannibal took the elephants over the Alps, surely we could get a form over the barbed wire. We went out to inspect the terrain. We'll have a go – It'll give us something to do – keep us out of mischief, we decided.

There was a lot of nattering over the next few days in the run-up to the Big Day. We studied the 'bunny run' – that was a run through the wire into the RAF compound. It was decided that the banjo wire could be the problem. The wooden bench would have to be carried from its present position in the hut, through the two doorways, turn left along the path which led to the latrine (not entering therein) and heading straight for the wire. The carriers were those with two reasonable legs. The bottom of the high wire was manipulated to allow the furniture removers to enter the banjo area with the nose of the bench. The legs of the bench were fixtures and about 15 inches long. Spike was still wearing his creation – imagine a fairly large flower pot, with a wide entry hole, slightly tapering to a small hole with a broom handle pushed through. He was on his back, the broomstick perpendicular, trying to avoid getting entangled in the wire, and all the time comments coming from the rest of us. 'Spike, mind where you're putting that thing! Ouch!' came a yell from someone he had speared. 'Mind where you're putting that fishing rod, Spike!'

Spike replied suitably. His fingers were busy.

How long this went on for I cannot say but eventually there were loud cheers as we all finally cleared the obstacles and the last man came out. We all lay spread-eagled on the dusty ground.

We finally got the bench into a spot near the touchline. There were no serious casualties.

The camp Commandant and his unmerry men arrived – under escort – and took their allotted places. I don't know what they paid for their seats – our medium of exchange was cigarettes. They were accompanied by the Senior British Officer. Then the players appeared, all wearing suitable attire. I don't remember if the colours were the official ones, but they all looked the part. Several players on each side were professional footballers in civvy street. Two I remember were Busby, an excellent full back who played for Coventry, and Jack Gardiner, who played for Luton both before and after the war. He was a half-back (these are the old players' positions). The goalkeeper for England came from the Channel Islands and was excellent.

When the whistle blew for half-time the pitch was taken

over by the pipe band, consisting of members of several famous regiments. They rendered their stirring music and were joined by the dancers from the Scottish regiments, all wearing national dress. Probably the kilts had been sent by the Red Cross, or some had managed to save theirs. The dancers included in their programme the sword dance with crossed swords. Of course the swords had to be replaced by wooden sticks – couldn't let the Germans think we were hostile! There were lots of cheers and yells, particularly when the pipers played *The Black Bear*.

The result of the match has long gone from my memory, but the event never will. Do you know, I have lost track of how we mad lot got that bench back to 11B. I have a sneaking suspicion that some of our friends in the camp took that privilege away. Well, they knew that we liked doing things for ourselves, but help was always there if required.

Life seemed a bit drearier after all the excitement of the match day and we had to return to our routine existence. Rumours had begun to circulate regarding possible repatriation. Often we were told, 'You'll be going home soon,' but our reply was tinged with disbelief: 'We have been on that road before!' We just carried on without any conviction that it could happen – even my margarine box didn't believe it.

I have just recalled a very fine episode, though I cannot be sure exactly where it occurred. Wherever it was, we had previously reminded our Swiss representatives that the Geneva Convention made provision for the inmates to be allowed a walk, under supervision. So it came to pass that we were instructed to be on parade to participate in this 'walk'. I think it only applied to leg amputees.

The parade set off, through the security gates and on to the open road, everybody happy, including the guards. It was a lovely day, the sunshine warm and the rolling countryside beautiful. All was right with the world – at least with this particular spot at this particular time. We had left the camp in columns of three, the crutches in no particular rhythm, the lads laughing and larking about and the guards tolerant.

We had been proceeding along the tree-lined road for some time. The trees had been planted in the grass verge some yards from the road, far enough for passers-by to be unable to distinguish what type of trees they were, but now they were close to the edge and some branches were overhanging the road with – APPLES!

Up went one crutch from somewhere, then another and another and more. The guards began shouting and waving their arms about. I was fully expecting some crutches to be growing on the trees if they got lodged in the branches. The Jerries were behaving like a line of rugby players, jumping up with arms outstretched in an effort to break the upward flight of a crutch – without success, poor chaps.

The column was still moving forward, if somewhat slowly. The situation was beginning to turn nasty, the guards dashing hither and thither trying to foil this attack on their fruit trees. Our lot, of course, like overgrown schoolboys, were revelling in the situation. Now the guards were rattling on their rifles, sending the message that they were going to open fire. I wondered if they had any ammo in the rifles, or if the rattling was a sham.

At this point we were approaching a sharp bend in the road. In the distance, from around the bend, came the sound of the army marching song, '*Wir marschieren gegen England*'. The singing grew louder the nearer the troops came. The attacks on the apple trees stopped; we were an untidy formation, but still in a column of three.

Quietly someone said, 'March to attention, lads.'

Amazingly there was immediate response – in line, pick up dressing – and at the same time crutches took the place of oars – in-out, in-out, in-out. The only suggestion had been to march to attention, but now we were replicas of the old galleys propelled by oars in-out, in-out. It must have been some sight! We were now entering the bend in the road and the leaders of the German column were just rounding it. With one voice, and without any command, came a blast of 'There'll always be an England, as long as Scotland's there!' We were still going in-out, in-out, in-out. As the column rounded the bend they saw us, bits and pieces of men, ancient galleys bearing down on them. Their singing tailed away, their marching became disorganised, untidy, their faces dropped. The galleys carried on in-out, in-out, in-out. 'There'll always be an England, as long as Scotland's there.'

We were NEVER allowed another walk.

The day-to-day routine went on with little variation. Sometimes we played, or tried to play, bridge. Some of the lads played it most days and for the best part of the day. Sometimes there would be a yell that someone had bid a grand slam and an interested audience would gather round and watch. There was no talking during play – simply not done. But when the hand had been played there would be an inquest on every move.

The college was going from strength to strength. The hut had been divided into rooms and more books were becoming available through the Red Cross. The college insignia and motto had been accepted by Oxford University. If it was a fine, warm day, Milner and I would probably do some swotting. Our favourite position was sitting in a large ditch a few yards from the hut. It had a flat bottom and nicely sloping sides, one of which made a back rest, the other propped the feet up. Some of the inmates were very fitness conscious, walking round and round the compound perimeter, pretending perhaps that they were on the deck on a liner at sea. Well, the imagination had to be exercised too.

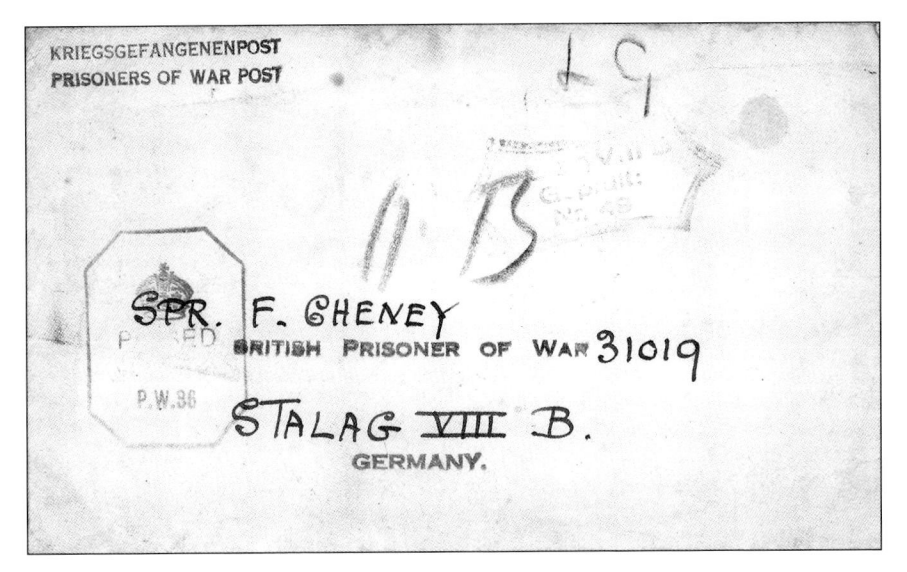

SPR. F. CHENEY
BRITISH PRISONER OF WAR 31019
STALAG VIII B.
GERMANY.

Postal Address 1941-43

The Runners 1939

Ron Varney and Vic Phillips           Frank Cheney and Vic Phillips

## BLETCHLEY MAN MISSING.

Sapper Frank Cheney, aged 21 years, only son of Mr. and Mrs. J. Cheney, of "Woodstock," Stoke Road, Water Eaton, has been reported missing. He is in the Royal Engineers and is well known in Bletchley as an athlete and a former member of the 1st Bletchley Co. B.B. and the B.B. Old Boys Football Club.

## THESE BLETCHLEY BOYS ARE SAFE

## Homes Made Happy This Week

### PREVIOUSLY "MISSING"—NOW "PRISONERS"

Bletchley homes have been made happy this week, with official notifications that men previously reported missing, are prisoners of war.

Frank Cheney, son of Mr. and Mrs. Cheney, Water Eaton, had been missing for three months and his parents had almost given up hope. On Wednesday, however, they received news that Frank is wounded, in hospital at Lille. He has had his foot amputated. It is coincidal that his father lost a leg in the last war.

Mr. and Mrs. G. Green, of 124, Western Road, Bletchley, received a card on Monday direct from their eldest son, Gnr. George Leslie Green, who is a prisoner in Germany at a camp known as Stalag. The card stated that he was "very well indeed."

Gnr. William Percival Adney, of 25, Osborne Street, Bletchley, is also a prisoner at Stalag VIIIB. Mrs. Adney has heard direct from her husband. The card said "I am well, a prisoner of war in Germany, and I am comfortable." Gnr. Adney was in the 226 Battery 57th Anti-Tank Corps.

Mrs. Plumb, of 28, Brooklands Road, Bletchley, has heard from her husband, John H. Plumb, who was reported missing on July 13th. The last communication from him was a Field Card from France on June 2nd. The card, written in ink, is dated June 18th, and there is nothing else on it to show where it came from. It reads, "I hope you and all the folks at home are well. I have been admitted into hospital and am now doing well. Please do not worry. I am sorry I have been a long time in writing, but I hope to write often now. Please do not write until I send an address. Cheerio! God bless you all." Signaller Plumb, is a son of Mr. and Mrs. J. W. Plumb, of 27, George Street Bletchley.

Mrs. Warren Wise, of Little Paxton, St. Neots, has received an official notice which states that her son is a prisoner of war. Cpl. Jack Wise is the only son of the late Mr. Warren Wise, who for many years practised as a dentist in Bletchley.

Cuttings from local Bletchley paper, 1940.

Cheney 2nd patient, left, front row, Dulag IXC Bad Salza.

Sick bay on Rouen Racecourse.

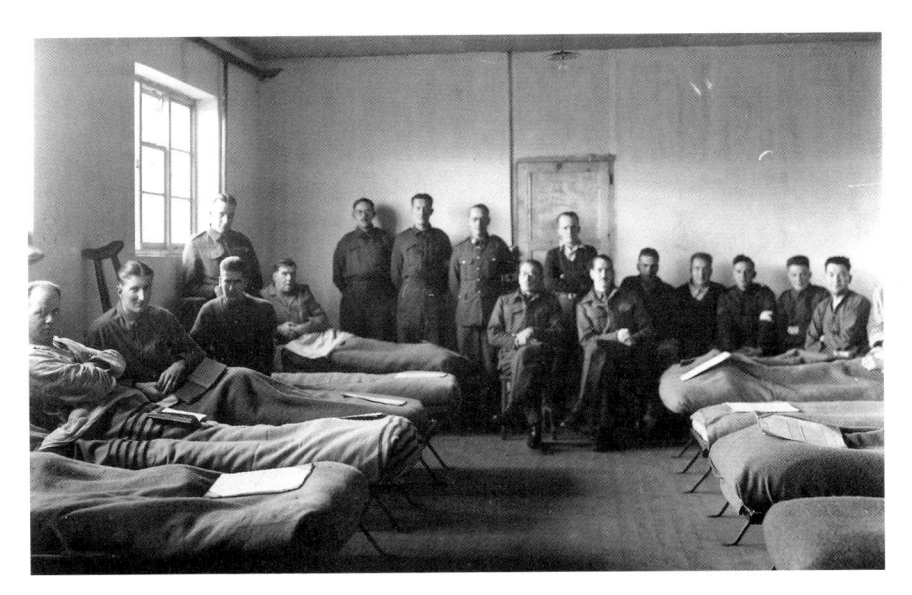

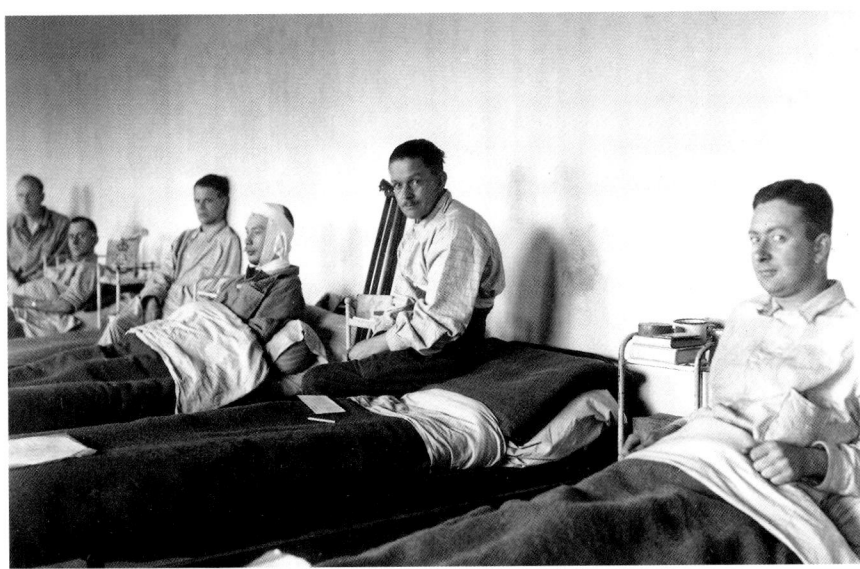

R.A.M.C. Medical orderlies - captured on camera!

S.S. *Drottningholm*

Boys and 'girls' of the concert party. Harry, 2nd left, is Harry 1st left below.

The three Harrys.

Clarence Aubert of Jersey, C.I.

Tutors of Stalag VIIIB College.

---

**WAR ORGANISATION OF THE BRITISH RED CROSS SOCIETY and ORDER OF ST. JOHN OF JERUSALEM.**

11.2.43

To ...SPR. F. Cheney 31019...

The following books were despatched to you by B. H. BLACKWELL LTD / W. J. BRYCE on the ...5th... of ...Feb..., 1943. A postcard for your acknowledgement is enclosed in the parcel. Please note on it if the entire contents have reached you. If not, please state which books were missing. **The books may be some months in transit.**

Contanseau: Pocket French Dictionary
C. Storey: Apprenons le mot juste
Graded Studies for free Composition
Grammaire Francaise: Berthon

To:- Spr. Frank CHENEY
31019 Stalag VIII.B.

Order 24814
Books some months in transit.

E. Herdman

The New Bodleian Library
Oxford

Secretary, Educational Books Section
**PRISONERS OF WAR DEPARTMENT**

Usual delivery time - six months or more.

The college crest as registered at Oxford.

'Ma' from Lille, Madame Germaine Holland.

Discharged!
No demob suit - only a khaki suit.

## DISCHARGE CERTIFICATE.
(If this Certificate is lost no duplicate can be obtained.)

Army Form B108J

Army Number: 1910671
Surname: CHENEY
Christian Names: Frank
Effective Date of Discharge: 16 April 1944
Corps from which Discharged: **ROYAL ENGINEERS.**
Total Service: Years: Four   Days: 100
Rank on Discharge: SAPPER
Cause of Discharge: **CEASING TO FULFIL ARMY PHYSICAL REQUIREMENTS**
Para: 390 (XVI) K. R. 1940

Campaigns: & Service Abroad,
B.E.F. FRANCE, 30-1-40 To 22-6-40,

Medals:

Military Conduct: Exemplary.

Signature and Rank Officer i/c Records.

Date: 21 March 1944   Place: **BRIGHTON.**

3012239

(20584) Wt.45638/182 500,000 1/42 A.& E.W.Ltd. Gp.698 Forms/B108J/1.

That also applied to our meals. Our daily bread ration reached one loaf of German ersatz bread to be shared between as many as 17 men. There were frequent rows as to who had the largest piece. At times violence flared and a referee had to intervene. All sorts of schemes and devices were concocted to ensure fair division. One rule was that each of the 'shareholders' took turns in cutting the required pieces. If a 'measuring stick' could be found, the overall dimensions, length, depth, width and any other peculiarities were noted and every piece was marked out, the cutter attempting to keep to the marks. The bread cut, playing cards were then brought into play. Cards would be chosen and laid face down against each piece, and a similar set extracted, shuffled by different persons and then dealt to the people participating. That done, the recipient could then take the piece corresponding to the card he held. Hunger brings out the worst in people.

The soup was mainly water, the other ingredients being of two kinds, rarely appearing together. One was German pineapple chunks (chef's special), squares of swede, the other was sauerkraut in the form of cabbage cut into strips and scattered in the liquid. It was like winning the lottery with these strips of cabbage stuff spaced out like railway stations in the desert. The pièce de résistance was spuds boiled in their overcoats, two or three depending on size. Seconds? Not on your nelly!

Individual parcels were restricted to so many per person. As I was employed by the London Midland and Scottish Railway Company, they relieved my parents of that responsibility. I think the quota was one parcel in three months. If you wished to have something that was not in the customary list of requirements, the parent could ask the railway people to include it. We went through a phase of being inundated with lice. I thought it would be useful if we could receive some Keatings Powder, which used to be advertised before the war as the thing for disposing of these creatures, so I asked my father if he would pass on the request for some of the exterminator.

A few months later a parcel appeared which contained the powder, so of course we had to try it out. It was not difficult to catch the things. After the round-up we opened the canister of powder, popped them into it and put the lid back on. We gave them a couple of days to develop into whatever they should, then opened the cage. There they were, as happy as lice in powder, getting fat! Back went the lid and they were left to enjoy their internment and the pleasure of the powder pot for another longer spell. After a week it was opening time again. What had happened? Had they gone wherever good lice go? Had they got any bigger? Were they like miniature elephants without tusks? Had they turned cannibal with only one remaining? The lid came off, and there they were munching as though their lives depended upon it. A decision had to be made as to their future. This was a drastic situation; this called for a Cabinet meeting, nothing less. The meeting was held, and the Wise Men of Lamsdorf decided that they must go. The window was opened, the lid was again removed and from their snug little home they were evicted. The whole lot – powder, lice and canister – were all cast to the four winds.

We returned to the ancient tried and trusted method of extermination – a flame.

Lice caused an epidemic of typhus in the Russian compound. It was so bad that the camp medical staff had suffered great losses and an appeal was made for volunteer medics to go to their assistance. Two of our orderlies volunteered. Some time later news arrived that they had perished. There are very brave people about.

One of our medical people had been a cinema organist before the war. Large cinemas installed electric organs to provide a musical interval in the programme. These organs, of which the most famous was probably the Wurlitzer, could produce, in the hands of an expert organist, music representing the instruments of a full orchestra. The instrument was stored below the floor at the front of the auditorium, and when the performance was due the player, seated at the organ, would slowly rise to the level of the audience. Our orderly could also play the accordion, and though very small, the instrument produced good music. One of our German guards also played this instrument. I think they conversed about music and musical instruments through our interpreter and the German allowed his prisoner to play his accordion, for a short time at first, but later, perhaps after he had obtained permission, he came back and we had some good entertainment from them both.

I mentioned that at the entrance to our hut, 11B, we had a stove for heating purposes. This was an unusual construction, looking like a tiled box from ground level to roof. There was a 'fire-box' at ground level, and somewhere in the box arrangement there must have been a 'feeder hole' for the fuel, but at this moment, after 60 years, my memory has 'downloaded'.

Well now, like me, many people had no cap badge representing the regiment or corps that they belonged to. Fags were in short supply and a drag had to be carefully restricted. Isn't there a saying that necessity is the mother of invention? The lads got thinking – they had lots of time to do it – saw the firebox glowing, and one could almost hear the rust being chipped away from the memory.

'Ever done any metal moulding?' The question came from the hidden depths of the hut.

'Yeah,' from somebody.

'That's it! Cap badges! We've got it!'

The search was on for metal buttons, wood for moulding boxes, suitable soil and all the materials that could and would be used. Having gathered the materials they started work on the production line. French army buttons were decided on as the material to melt down. I was trying to remember what was used as the smelting pot, but it eludes me. It had to be strong to stand the heat required, but some receptacle was found because I saw the buttons bubbling in the pot. It took a steady hand to pour the molten metal into the casting hole, and it took a while to achieve success, but the finished casting was a fair representation of the original.

Eventually I forked up my ten fags and acquired a badge of the Royal Engineers. My wife had it attached to her ATS shoulder bag for years at Bletchley Park and later postings. I think its present resting place is in a spare wardrobe. It is still attached to the bag – and has been for over 50 years.

There was something not quite right with my amputation stump. It was unusually painful and, I thought, a little swollen, so I approached Don, one of our orderlies. They were all excellent. If they thought something was affecting anyone they would investigate. The painful swelling was discussed and it was decided that there would be further developments – and there were. In a couple of weeks the swelling had grown in size. It was an abscess. It could be compared to a large bunch of juicy grapes. I could not straighten my knee, it was permanently bent.

It was decided that a visit to the camp hospital was necessary, so off we went. The hospital doctor, a colonel, had been with the prisoners since Dunkirk

'Right, we'll deal with that,' he said on viewing my bunch of grapes, so a bed was found for me and the 'operation' took place, but not before I was given an injection. I was told to count: one – two – three – fo— I could feel the doctor's two hands around my knee applying pressure with the thumb and fingers just below my kneecap and straightening the leg. Then I lost consciousness.

When the orderly was changing the dressing the next day I mentioned that as I was going under I could feel the pressure that the doctor was applying.

'As you were going,' he said, 'and at the point you're talking about, the pressure burst the abscess and the pus and blood went everywhere. The doctor was showered – and everyone else within range.' What you might call a bloody mess.

Spring was beginning to turn to summer and the temperature was slowly rising. One day the SBO received an order from the German Commandant to the effect that as the German army returned their greatcoats to the stores, to be reissued in the autumn, we should do the same. Well, that caused it: A quiet revolution. 'We're not going to hand our coats in' (at least that's a polite version of what was said). An open forum followed and it was agreed that we should put our case to the Commandant that the British Army *did not* hand their greatcoats in for storage, and we were British Army. We were also, in lots of cases, badly wounded soldiers, and there were various other points which have escaped me at the moment. However, our representative gained an audience with the Germans and the result was that the German command would carry out an inspection on a certain day. 'Good. We'll show 'em!' (an expurgated version of the comments). Out came the greatcoats (90 per cent of them were a supplement to our meagre blankets), button sticks, makeshift polish – probably ash from the fire. Button sticks (to avoid getting metal polish on the coat material) were in limited supply – and were the property of the medical orderlies – but this was action stations. All hands to the pumps!

I believe I have already mentioned that a wooden rail ran along the centre of the hut with wooden pegs fixed at regular intervals. On these the greatcoats were now displayed with military precision, shining buttons fastened, sleeves folded back and tucked into the belt, which was tightened, giving a smooth presentation about 12 inches wide. Imagine the buttons gleaming on the double-breasted greatcoats - a line of 50 guards standing to attention ready for inspection. There was no visible reaction from the German inspecting officers – but we kept our greatcoats.

In the summer of 1943 rumours began to circulate to the effect that we were going to be repatriated. Of course we replied to this with great disbelief. 'We've heard that one before! Tell us another one!' We were going to be supplied with artificial limbs by the Swiss and that was two years ago – we were still waiting for both events. After the 1941 trip on which we *nearly* made it home we were again visited by another team from Switzerland. They again took details as to which country we would go to *if* we were repatriated. Most of us said the same as before. I said England, the Scots said Scotland. In our midst we had a party of six who had served in the defence of Norway at Narvik in April 1940, together with the Navy. Their senior member was a platoon sergeant major. They had a quick discussion before delivering their required destination and one remarked, 'Let's have a change – tell them Australia, so they did! We were at this stage 'disbelievers' and had no faith in the stories that we were going home soon.

Our days drifted along with little objective: listening to the latest 'scoop' regarding the latest 'racket' and the racketeers, and giving assistance if we possibly could to people trying to stock up and get out of Lamsdorf to a working party, with the main object to escape. We were stuck, but the 'Bits and

Pieces' were always having a chuckle at something or someone. Our hut, both ends, was always full with people from other compounds, and people who came into the camp from working parties usually found their way to us.

The fact was that most of us only thought about today. I for instance had my mother and father to think of, I had no other ties, but some chaps had families and children they had never seen. In these circumstances all thoughts encourage depression and some went insane but had no help from our captors. We had a lad with us whom we called Dick. He was in his early twenties, like most of us, and had lost his left arm at the shoulder. For most of the day he sat forlorn with his chin on his chest, showing no interest when we tried to speak to him. One of our padres used to spend hours with Dick, trying patiently to interest him in something, anything, but to no avail.

While on this subject, there was at one time information traversing the camp that one of the patients in Block D, which housed people with mental disorder, had been exercising his toy dog. Several unfortunate persons had reverted to their childhood and had toys on wheels, as young children do. He had just wandered around but was now in line with the perimeter fencing. The trip wire was first, about eight yards from the seven-foot barbed-wire fence. He had crossed the trip wire with his 'dog' when the guard spotted him and challenged him. He didn't stop, just continued. The guard fired. He carried on and began to climb up the wire. He was hit, according to the report, several times. The information was that the body was left hanging on the barbed wire for four days before permission was granted to take it away.

The population of Lamsdorf was growing rapidly. With the Allied Forces advancing in Italy, the prisoners captured in various Mediterranean battles were brought in to Upper

Silesia. We had no radios – officially – and now these people were able to fill in the parts we knew nothing about. The talk was still persisting that 'us lot' were going home, though we still didn't agree. It was August 1943 and I think that many of us wondered how we would fare through another German winter. Our food ration was not equal to the German army rations, which is what the Geneva Convention stipulated, but we did know that our rations were not as bad as those of the Russians. We could complain about our circumstances, but the Jerries were going to feed their own people before the prisoners they had captured. A number of us quietly thought that living conditions would deteriorate and we would be lucky to survive. That would be during our serious five minutes of thought on the future, but after that the thoughts had to be dispelled and replaced with a smile on the face. Too many dismal thoughts and long faces wouldn't get us anywhere.

My father, who had lost his right leg in the 1914–18 war, must have surmised the situation, though I don't think I gave any inkling in my correspondence to my parents. Our allowance for correspondence was very small, possibly one letter-card and two or three post card types, I forget the exact number. He used to write every Sunday where possible and he would finish by saying something like, 'It's a long lane that has no turning' or 'Keep your pecker up', or 'Every cloud has a silver lining'.

I am not quite sure of the circumstances leading up to our leaving Lamsdorf Stalag VIIIb. I think we may have been given a couple of days' notice of our departure. There was a strong belief in the camp that we were going to be repatriated, and among ourselves, the participants, there was hope that this was true. We gathered up our worldly wealth and I placed mine in my margarine box. Some months previously I had received, through the Red Cross, a number of text books. I wanted to study for the Matriculation Examination. Although I wanted to take them all with me, it was impossible, so I asked around among my friends who would like them, or at least pass them on to the college library to help other people.

My friend Lionel Wickson from Leighton Buzzard said he would like the books. There is rather an unlikely story of our meeting in VIIIb. I have to go back to 1927–28. I was a member of Fenny Stratford Wolf Cubs, who used to meet at the old vicarage, at the junction of Vicarage Road and Aylesbury Street, and one of the other boys in the pack was Lionel. We got on very well and were friends outside the Cubs, but after about three years Lionel and his family moved to Leighton Buzzard and we lost contact. I have mentioned that the prisoners from Dieppe occupied the next compound before any others and could be seen by us through the windows of our hut. On this particular day several of them were in the compound kicking a football around, and I said to myself, 'That chap looks familiar,' but something else happened and I forgot all about it.

Some time later several of us were sitting around our table when suddenly a head and shoulders bobbed through the array of overcoats hanging on their pegs. Immediately I said, 'Lionel Wickson – what are you doing here?' or something equally daft.

He had apparently been talking to Sergeant Bill Purcell, from Bletchley, who had been dealing with people going out on working parties, and in the course of conversation the usual question arose: 'Where do you come from?' (Well, I'll be Buzzard!) We saw each other very often after that but I am sorry to say we have never met in England. It's a funny old world.

The only item of cutlery that most of us had was a spoon. The Germans confiscated all knives above a certain size so a spoon became a universal tool, rather like a Nelson Knife. We had acquired tin openers through our individual parcels. When we received our first Red Cross parcels containing tinned food, we had no openers and this caused a great deal of 'brainracking' as to how to extract the food from the tin. I can't remember how it was done – perhaps you can think of a way. The other item of importance was some sort of container for liquids. We had received Red Cross parcels from Canada and among the goodies that they contained was a larger than usual tin of powdered milk, labelled KLIM. The empty tin was converted into a marvellous mug, with another piece of tin ingeniously formed into a handle. These two items were essential to one's wellbeing and survival. The spoon had one side of the bowl slightly sharpened to enable small and not too tough items to be cut. That applied mainly to food items from the parcel tins. I used to keep the spoon about my person and the tin mug handy – one never knew when they might be needed.

The Moving Day arrived. The camp was buzzing: there were people outside the compound in the road, on both sides of which squaddies were standing in small groups talking, and occasionally glancing towards the interior of our compound to check on what, if anything, was happening. I have no idea of the time, except that it was morning – perhaps between ten and eleven. I cannot remember whether we, our hut, were first or last to go, but suddenly it was our turn to leave our 'little grey home in the East'.

Through the doors for the last time, turn right past Mildew's and my seat in the ditch and on towards the end of the compound, then right again, and the gate of the compound was open. Outside in the road were crowds of men, cheering. We, the outgoing personnel, were now in single file and as we went through the gate, as if by magic, the crowd cleared a way, just wide enough for single-line traffic to pass.

There was shouting, cheering, backslapping and occasionally 'for they are jolly good fellows!' It was like running the gauntlet, but no whips – backslapping and handshaking all the way to the main gate. The whole camp must have been in that formation lining the way for us. There must have been about fifteen thousand cheering people. What a send-off.

# 10

## *Return Ticket*

I went through the open gates, the first time since that freezing cold February day when we arrived. The German guards were on duty just the other side of the gate the free side – and army trucks were waiting in line. We were ushered into the lorries and when they were full we set off to – we did not know where. We eventually arrived at a railway siding and the train was waiting, the engine with steam up ready for the off.

We got out of the vehicles with some difficulty, straightened ourselves up, and in our own time set off for the train. We were directed into a carriage and then a compartment, corridor stock and good, six to a compartment – two up aloft, two on seats for medium-sized 'bods' and two on the floor. In cases of emergency the volunteers up aloft had difficulty in extracting themselves from the mesh of the rack, and the 'ground floor' went to their aid. Sometimes it was all hands required to prevent injury.

In its own time and when fully loaded, the engine, with a chug and a *sh-h-h* of steam, set off. The question was, where were we going? Were we going home, as the whole of Lamsdorf thought we were, or were we to appear at another camp? The train chugged on through the night. I am unable to recall if we were fed, or if we had any food at all, but next morning we did have some food – no, not eggs and bacon, but any food is food. Unfortunately, it comes in many guises. Some of the guards were on the train but they seemed more relaxed than on previous excursions. They even allowed us to go to the 'little boys' room' without the usual escort.

For the want of something better to do, our compartment tried to deduce which way we were heading – north, east, south or west. Of course the train was twisting around like a corkscrew and that made it difficult to assess the direction. Someone tried the sliding door and it slid open. No guard. No, put that thought back in the pigeonhole! The train was moving along at a steady speed and the gradual increase in the number of buildings was changing the terrain from rolling landscape to industrial and residential areas. Then a station, Breslau, we were going *north*! Now that really put the cat among the pigeons. Where were we heading? There was lots of speculation but no information at all. Still, it was a wonderful game, and all would surely be revealed at some future date.

We wondered what had become of the guards. There appeared to be only a few and they showed no interest in us at all. The train was rolling along at a steady pace, not trying to break any records. The next station of any note that I remember was Poznan. The lads had tumbled to a new wheeze. When the train stopped at a convenient point and looked like being there some time, out would come a receptacle and some tea leaves, to be taken out of the coach on to the track and along to the engine driver. *'Heiss' Wasser, bitte. Zwei Zigaretten.'* The driver usually obliged. The receptacle was placed under the water reject pipe of the engine, the driver applied the right pressure and the hot water came out at a gentle pace. Sometimes it came out with a rush but he would be watching and stop the flow immediately. Can't beat a good brew-up!

Of course during these trips the engine driver and his mate collected quite a few fags and some of the lads who had picked up a bit of the German language engaged the footplatemen in brief conversation. Gradually, from titbits of information regarding place names, it was decided that we were heading for the Isle of Rügen, to a place called Sassnitz. It was beginning to look as if we could be repatriated – but don't get too excited yet.

The train was still rolling along nicely, past Stettin, with the steady clinking of the carriage passing over the joins in the track like the good old steam trains used to do before the installation of longer-length rails. The countryside was varied; we were in Poland and the people were working in the fields. It was October, and a busy time for people working on the land.

We eventually reached our destination, said to be a naval camp, and not far from the Isle of Rügen. We tried to keep our little gang together but it proved impossible. We were being ushered into huts, and as one hut received its capacity holding, say 20, the intake was stopped and moved on to the next one. By now it was nearly dark. I was in a hut with lots of strangers, only one or two from VIIIb. There appeared to be no restriction on moving about outside, so I resolved to find out where the rest of the gang was located. I started off, working around to the right and shouting 'Collins' as loudly as I could, past one hut and another, and after what seemed like a two-week holiday, I returned to my new residence without success. I stayed in there a while and as there was nothing happening there, I decided to try the moonlight again. I got outside and was standing about like a lost bridegroom at a wedding when I made up my mind to move again. I had not gone above a dozen steps when I bumped into Collins. He was housed in the next hut – the first of my waking calls. We then had a recap on the past hours until it was time to turn in.

The next morning we set off for Sassnitz in our usual mode of transport. After what seemed a short ride we reached our objective and entered the train which was on board the train ferry to Sweden. In due course, after our transfer from the Germans to the Swedish Red Cross, the skipper raised the anchor. There was that marvellous feeling that I always get when I am on board a vessel pulling away from the dock, the engine running: 'Let go for'ard', the line comes in, the ship's nose comes away from the dock and she's swinging round on the aft line: 'Cast off!' We were away. Do you know what? WE WERE GOING HOME!

It was a lovely morning in the last part of October. The sun was shining on a slight sea, and now our vessel was under way we could go up on deck. I think everyone had the feeling that we had won the football pools. (There was no lottery in those days.) At that moment life was very good and we thought we represented the 'idle rich', sitting on deck and puffing our baccy. There was much banter among the lads, on a ship in the Baltic, bound for the Swedish port of Malmo. The scene was enhanced by the ladies of the Red Cross passing round packed-lunch boxes full of goodies to eat, which were very gratefully received.

After all these years I am unable to say how long the crossing of the Baltic from Sassnitz took, but I think we reached Malmo some time in the afternoon. However, we did arrive, and I can recall the ferry docking and the engine hooking up to the electric system, all most interesting for us to watch. I wonder if the ferry still operates on the same route now.

We had been travelling for a short period when a young Swedish lady put her head round the door and asked, 'Is there room for me?' Well, it's said that lightning doesn't strike twice. There was a chorus of 'Yes!' and she came in and took her seat in the middle of this bunch of – nice young men. Oh yes we were! I think we had forgotten what a young lady looked like. It had been over three years since many had been in a lady's company. The poor girl was bombarded with questions about what would happen at Malmo. Would we change trains? She played excellent cricket and dealt with the bowling very well. After question time she tried to get us to sing. It's funny how Continentals always think that we want to sing – it must be all those football supporters. Anyway, she was asked if she knew any English songs, and would she sing the first part to see if we knew the song. Of course we were absolutely rotten. We let the girl sing, and when she stopped everyone cheered and clapped and coaxed her to sing some more – without success. While writing this I can still visualise that nice young lady in the middle, seated with those young men, and all having fun and enjoying the company. She must have been in the compartment for nearly an hour when, looking at her watch, she said 'It's time I said goodbye.' What gentlemen there were stood up (it was all of them actually) and waved goodbye.

Among the many questions asked, she had told us that our ultimate destination was Gothenburg, where we would board the ship to go home.

We reached Malmo and after a short stay left to continue our journey to Gothenburg. The rest of the trip, as far as I can recall, was uneventful. During our journey on the train we had been visited by the Swedish Red Cross gentlemen and given labels stating our names and the allocation number of our accommodation on board ship. This had to be kept until we were requested to pass it over in exchange for our living quarters on the sea voyage.

# 11

## SS Drottningholm

The train duly arrived in Gothenburg and chugged along the quay to the landing stage beside our ship, the *SS Drottningholm*. There were many willing hands to assist us to alight from the train and escort us to wherever we had been allocated. I don't remember my deck number but it was very high up, because I finished up in a two-berth stateroom – with all mod cons. I was joined by another chap, a complete stranger, but we introduced ourselves and in the course of conversation discussed the sleeping arrangements. As I said, it was a two-berth cabin, with an upper and a lower berth. My new acquaintance stated his preference for the upper berth, which suited me, so that situation was quickly settled.

The stateroom was fascinating to me. I had come from a prison camp with only the bare essentials to what was, by contrast, a miniature palace. Everything was gleaming, the white bedding, paintwork, brasswork – I don't think it was gold. The floor covering was soft to the foot, the whole bloody marvellous.

My fellow traveller and I got cleaned up and he left to find his mates. I found Collins, who was housed not far away in similar surroundings, and we sallied forth to explore the ship, like good landlubbers do. John and I agreed about the transformation that had taken place in our living standards. No amount of cash could buy this. We even had a loo with a handle to flush. (Why does the Navy refer to the lavatory as the 'heads'?)

We had to present ourselves in the dining room at a given time; no queues, just take yourself. There were, as far as I remember, no menus – well, we didn't like menus anyway. Food, Glorious Food was our favourite (but not spuds boiled in their overcoats, thank you very much). The food was great. The only thing I can recall about it is that the chef produced a wonderful fish dish. We had forgotten what a fish looked like. Another thing, the food was served on plates, not any old bits of stuff like dixies and Klim tins, and we didn't have to do the washing up.

The ship's captain made an announcement over the intercom that the ship would be putting to sea to test the ship's compass the next day, and the next day as promised she raised steam and we left our berth at the landing stage and took to the open water It was magnificent weather, sunshine and a flattish sea, and we just pottered about doing whatever was necessary to test a compass. What that was I don't know because no further information was given, so it was assumed that the compass knew its job. However, it was great to be out and in the fresh air away from our prison surroundings.

On our return to port, we were informed that a member of the Swedish Royal Family would be visiting the ship at a certain time on the next day. More information would follow when details were known, I was on deck around midmorning when I heard that the niece of Lord Mountbatten was on board. I had found an English newspaper somewhere and was reading this when the Royal Lady and a small escort came towards me. As they approached I brought the newspaper down to one side and did my best to stand to attention on a peg leg. The lady walked past with a slight nod of the head and proceeded along the deck to where several chaps were standing. She stopped and enquired if anyone

76

was in the Navy. One man was, and he was then asked if he had served with her uncle, Earl Mountbatten. 'No, Ma'am,' he replied, and after a few more questions she continued on her rounds. I wish I could remember the lady's rank: she certainly showed a great interest in our personnel, the 'Bits and Pieces'. Her visit also left a memorable impression on us. Since our arrival on Swedish soil we had been treated with great cordiality and care.

During late afternoon news came that the two ships transporting the German repats would be arriving next day, probably in the morning. We had no idea how many persons the ships were carrying, we would have to wait and see.

The next morning I was on deck as usual busy doing nothing – in fact one might say I was extremely busy. I was on the starboard side (right-hand side to all landlubbers) when I spied two large ships crossing our bow. Lots of interest was being shown by all the other personnel who happened to be on our deck. There was a buzz of excitement. They were the hospital ships, the *Atlantis* and the *Empress of Russia*. There were people on the decks, possibly more on the decks of the *Empress of Russia*, as I understood from information received long after this that she had been converted into a hospital ship in rather a hurry. The *Atlantis* was said to have sailed with 788 German sick and wounded and civilian internees.

There was isolated waving to us from both those ships but I did not see anyone waving from our deck in return. In fact one could have said, 'There was a deathly hush in the close tonight', or something very similar.

We had been on board the *Drottningholm* for several days and, with the arrival of the two ships, was there *still* a possibility that something could happen to stop the exchange again? There was a war on, and governments contain very funny people at times. Most of the chaps were very optimistic with ''Course we're going home!' but those of us who had been in the situation of waiting for the boat before were not quite so certain.

A day or so later those doubts were dispelled by the actions of the ship's crew. They were rechecking equipment for a sea trip. The engines were running; up came the anchor. The captain gave instructions and his officers carried out his orders and *SS Drottningholm* eased herself away from the dock.

A few blasts on the horn. Thank you, Sweden.

> A life on the ocean wave,
> A life on the rolling sea,
> We'll soon be home again
> For a lovely cup of tea!
> We hope!

The ship slid quietly away from the quayside and out into the main bay and followed the other two vessels in line astern. I believe that's what it's called when ships are in single file with a distance between them. I think we left Gothenburg on 19th October 1943 and probably travelled through the Skagerrak. I remember passing through what appeared to be a great number of islands and some of these had what could have been ack-ack guns. They were guns of some sort anyway. Round the foot of Norway, part Lindesnes and a mile or two from the Norwegian coast, the three ships would have been clearly visible at night. The *Atlantis* was leading, all white with large red crosses on her sides and a broad green band, floodlit; the *Empress of Russia* was in the middle, bearing large red crosses and floodlighting, and finally the *Drottningholm*, with white-painted hull, large red crosses and floodlit. A few miles past Egersund we left the Norwegian coast and made straight for the gap north of Scotland, that route being taken by the *Atlantis* and the *Empress*, down to Liverpool. We, the *Drottningholm*, travelled down the eastern coastline to Leith, where we docked on 23rd October 1943 though I can't remember what time. While we were on board and travelling with the other vessels, talking amongst ourselves, we wondered how many U-boat captains had us in their periscopes. That we shall never know. In the daytime it was lovely sailing and as I remember the weather was excellent. The grub was excellent too. There must be something in this cruising lark!

It was 23rd October and we were approaching Leith. We were still some distance away from the quay but sirens, hooters and whistles could be heard, and of course the nearer we got the louder the noise. We had to stand off because passengers were taken ashore by tender.

We were soon tied up and made secure and unloading began. The noise was now focussed on the unloading tenders and I think it was even greater than when we were on board ship. Several tenders were plying between ship and shore and each had returned several times, but those of us from hut 11B had stayed until we were obliged to leave the ship. Finally we clambered into the tenders and were delivered to the shore. The noise was deafening. A great Scottish welcome!

Volunteers from several organisations were waiting to act as porters. I thanked the lady who wanted to relieve me of my margarine box with a 'No, thank you very much. I think I can manage.'

At that point I looked across at John Collins. Another lady was trying to relieve John of his treasures. He apparently had also declined the offer of assistance, but his lady wouldn't take no for an answer and they were having a tug-of-war with John's bag. Eventually John won; he carried it – but the lady walked beside him all along the walkway.

# 12

## *Home Station*

After a walk of some 70 yards or so we were ushered through a channel which eventually allowed only two persons through at a time. Two army officers were asking a few questions, one of which was, 'Have you escaped or tried to escape?' If the answer was yes, you were asked to 'step this way', and that was through another door. It so happened that the chap who was forming a twosome with me was Hamish Gunn – you remember about our meeting at Rouen and he said he would try to escape and had fitted a foot to his pylon leg. He was my opposite number and was invited to pass through the side door. I continued straight ahead.

How we reached Penicuik is somewhat hazy. Some sort of transport was involved and we arrived in gathering darkness. It seemed to be a very large army depot. Once there, we went into what I recall as Nissen huts. It was the usual stuff, an NCO indicating that so many must go in this one and 'you lot' in that one. I have forgotten how many to each hut. There we were, back in the Army!

A nice, friendly corporal 'read the lesson' and informed us that a 'welcome home' party was to be held in the dining hall at such and such an hour, and we were all guests of the camp, so would we all make ourselves at home and prepare for the feast. The nice corporal also told us where the dining hall was – up this way and across that way and you will probably be there.

So, we set off to find the dining hall. It was rather difficult because it was just about dark and of course black-out was in operation. Moving gingerly, we eventually found the door and entered the hall. Lots of lovely ATS girls were acting as hostesses and showing us to a seat. Do you know – but of course you don't because I haven't told you yet – silly me! Well, remember Hamish Gunn? I finished up sitting next to him.

Tea was started, lots of lovely GRUB, and lots of chat from the ladies, who wanted to know about our exploits. During the course of the meal they told us that after tea, and later in the evening when the tables had been cleared, the camp was holding a dance, and asked who of us would be going. Some said they would – I can't dance, don't ask me!

Tea over, we dispersed to our huts. They probably had numbers for recognition, I don't remember, but having found our 'stateroom' we of course entered. Lots of the chaps had already returned and were quizzing the corporal about camp security – 'How does one get out of here now that one is in?'

I tell you, you get out of one jail and straight into another one. Anyone got a 'get out of jail free' card?

What the lads really wanted to do was to find a pub. The nice corporal said, 'Well, there is a way out but it is extremely risky.'

The poor corporal! He wasn't to know he was talking to chaps who had been in 'extremely risky' situations before. He wasn't to know that they would be down at the opposite end of the compound visiting, four huts away from their lovely beds in Stalag VIIIb, when lights were extinguished and searchlights began to rake the compound. The only way back was to go to the washhouse in the middle of the hut and open the unsighted window which looked across parallel to the next hut, then *dive* through the open window to land very close to the next hut, and enter. This process had to be repeated until one arrived back home. Any sighting by the Germans would be announced by machine-gun fire.

Back to the nice corporal. He did continue his directions for the grand exit so they began their preparations. Chaps on crutches decided to try their luck. Obviously they had cats' eyes'! Me? I had a lovely quiet evening, talking to the nice corporal. The next day was full of reports from the 'Good Time Boys' regarding their night-time escapades. Some apparently managed to reach their objective, a pub, and were very well received and well supplied with drinks. They also managed to get back to the billet without getting nicked and without waking the sleeping personnel.

I think then that we were kitted out with new khaki suits in preparation for going on leave. I still had my ten-bob note. The next few days were spent in attending interviews, which revolved around how and where we were captured, the date, if possible, on which one was wounded, army unit, and suchlike information. Speaking to some of the interviewers afterwards, it seemed they were astounded at the number of people who were able to quote the date of their being injured. I have always remembered my date, 26th May 1940, in the afternoon, I think. We were also told when and how we would be sent on leave, the exact details of which elude me. What I do recall is the St John Ambulance people would be travelling with some of us and would join us in Edinburgh.

We were duly transported from Penicuik Camp to Edinburgh, where a lady officer of the St John Brigade introduced herself to me. She told me that she would be escorting me to London, and that we were to catch the overnight express from Edinburgh to London, travelling in a reserved compartment. She didn't say if we had any fellow travellers.

It was time to join the train and we were escorted to our compartment, I think in first class. The lady took her corner seat by the window with her back to the engine and made herself as comfortable as possible. I took the corner window seat opposite. There were the usual last-minute goodbyes from people parting from their friends, the engine whistle blowing, the train guard blowing his whistle in turn and getting a reply from up front, all clear, another whistle from the guard, a wave of the green flag. There was a *s-s-sh*, *s-s-sh*, and a cloud of steam, the drive wheels spinning, then a final whistle from the engine driver and we were chugging away from the platform – we were off!

My lady escort was very concerned that I should get some sleep and that I should put my leg along the unoccupied seat. By this time the express was speeding along and I didn't want to go to sleep, I wasn't tired, I was more interested in looking through the window at the passing countryside. At intervals we chatted and I tried to persuade my escort to rest. In the end I think she just fell quietly asleep.

We duly arrived at Kings Cross *on time*! We alighted from the train, to be met by another St John's officer, and after a wee chat as to which terminus I should go to, I departed to Euston, possibly by taxi, but anyway I arrived at Euston station.

It was funny being back on Euston forecourt. It seemed just the same as I remembered it, except that the public house that had stood on the corner of Drummond Street wasn't there. That was the pub where Dennis Atkins and I had half a pint before he left for Catterick and I went back to France. (After 60-odd years, he still owes me half a pint!)

I found the indicator board, discovered when the next train left for Bletchley, reached the platform – number eight, I think – passed through the ticket barrier, chose a compartment and seat, and was soon on my way – on the last bit of my journey. My train was one which had 'local' stock. From Euston the first stop was Watford, then all stations to Bletchley. The train seemed to take for ever, station after station lit by those very dim gas lights, but, of course, there was a war on. We reached Leighton Buzzard – not far to go now – the final lap.

We left Leighton and continued our clippity-clop past the Fletton Brickworks, reached the platform, passed the stairs and finally stopped. I was gathering myself together and had stood up facing the door, but before I could reach it the door burst open. There was a porter standing there.

'Are you …!' Before I could answer he fired a reprimand.

'Your mother's bin up here all night waiting for you! About time you got here! Where've you bin?'

He vanished as quickly as he had appeared.

Now the real battle for survival was about to begin.

# *Postscript*

All three athletes survived the war. Vic Phillips became a flying officer in the RAF, Ron Varney became a sergeant in the Army, serving in India. Frank Cheney became a sapper in the Royal Engineers travelling through Europe as POW 31019.
I was the only one to be permanently disabled.
There were no provisions for demobilisation in those days, and a long struggle ensued to gain qualifications, but finally, after years of evening studies with correspondence classes, I achieved membership of the Chartered Institute of Secretaries.
I married, in 1946, a member of the ATS formerly attached to the Intelligence Corps at Bletchley Park, later the Army Education Corps. We have a twin son and daughter, four grandchildren and two great-grandchildren. It is in response to constant prodding, not to say pestering, from the family that this story came to be written.